THE HUNDRED DRESSES

ISBN 979-11-91343-81-6 14740

Longtail Books

THE
HUNDRED
DRESSES

ELEANOR ESTES

ILLUSTRATED BY

LOUIS SLOBODKIN

WANDA

Today, Monday, Wanda Petronski was not in her seat. But nobody, not even Peggy and Madeline, the girls who started all the fun, **notice**d her **absence**.

Usually Wanda sat in the next to the last seat in the last **row** in Room 13. She sat in the corner of the room where the **rough** boys who did not make good **marks**

4

on their **report card**s sat; the corner of the room where there was most **scuffling** of feet, most **roars** of **laughter** when anything funny was said, and most mud and **dirt** on the floor.

Wanda did not sit there because she was rough and **noisy**. On the **contrary** she was very quiet and **rarely** said anything at all. And nobody had ever heard her laugh out loud. Sometimes she **twist**ed her mouth into a **crook**ed sort of smile, but that was all.

Nobody knew **exact**ly why Wanda sat in that seat **unless** it was because she came all the way from Boggins **Height**s, and her feet were usually **caked** with dry mud that she picked up coming down the country roads. Maybe the teacher liked to keep all the children who were **apt** to come in with dirty shoes in one corner of the room. But no one really thought much about Wanda Petronski once she was in the classroom. The time they thought about her was outside of school hours, at **noontime** when they were coming back to school, or in the morning early before school began, when groups of two or three or even

more would be talking and laughing on their way to the school **yard**.

Then sometimes they waited for Wanda—to have fun with her.

The next day, Tuesday, Wanda was not in school either. And nobody noticed her absence again, **except** the teacher and probably big Bill Byron, who sat in the seat behind Wanda's and who could now put his long legs around her empty desk, one on each side, and sit there like a frog, to the great **entertain**ment of all in his corner of the room.

But on Wednesday, Peggy and Maddie, who sat in the front row along with other children who got good marks and didn't **track** in a whole lot of mud, did notice that Wanda wasn't there. Peggy was the most popular girl in school. She was pretty; she had many pretty clothes and her **auburn** hair was **curly**. Maddie was her closest friend.

The reason Peggy and Maddie noticed Wanda's absence was because Wanda had made them late to school. They had waited and waited for Wanda—to have some fun with her—and she just hadn't come. They kept thinking she'd come any minute. They saw Jack Beggles running to school, his necktie **askew** and his cap at a **precarious tilt**. They knew it must be late, for he always managed to **slide** into his chair exactly when the bell rang as though he were making a **touchdown**. Still they waited one

minute more and one minute more, hoping she'd come.
But finally they had to **race** off without seeing her.

The two girls reached their classroom after the doors
had been closed. The children were **reciting** in **unison**

the Gettysburg Address,* for that was the way Miss Mason always began the **session**. Peggy and Maddie **slip**ped into their seats just as the class was saying the last lines . . .

"that these dead shall not have died in **vain**; that the **nation** shall, under God, have a new birth of freedom, and that **government** of the people, by the people, for the people, shall not **perish** from the earth."

★ Gettysburg Address 게티즈버그 연설. 미국 남북 전쟁이 진행되던 1863년 11월 19일, 격전지였던 펜실베이니아 주 게티즈버그에서 전사한 장병들의 영혼을 위로하는 추도식에서 미국의 16대 대통령 링컨이 한 연설.

THE DRESSES GAME

AFTER Peggy and Maddie stopped feeling like **intruder**s
in a class that had already begun, they looked across the
room and **notice**d that Wanda was not in her seat.
Furthermore her desk was **dust**y and looked as though

she hadn't been there yesterday either. Come to think of it, they hadn't seen her yesterday. They had waited for her a little while but had forgotten about her when they reached school.

They often waited for Wanda Petronski—to have fun with her.

Wanda lived way up on Boggins **Heights**, and Boggins Heights was no place to live. It was a good place to go and pick **wildflowers** in the summer, but you always **held your breath till** you got safely past old man Svenson's yellow house. People in the town said old man Svenson was no good. He didn't work and, worse still, his house and **yard** were **disgraceful**ly dirty, with **rusty tin** cans **strew**n about and even an old **straw** hat. He lived alone with his dog and his cat. **No wonder**, said the people of the town. Who would live with him? And many stories **circulate**d about him and the stories were the kind that made people **scurry** past his house even **in broad daylight** and hope not to meet him.

Beyond Svenson's there were a few small **scattere**d

frame houses, and in one of these Wanda Petronski lived with her father and her brother Jake.

Wanda Petronski. Most of the children in Room 13 didn't have names like that. They had names easy to say, like Thomas, Smith, or Allen. There was one boy named Bounce, Willie Bounce, and people thought that was funny but not funny in the same way that Petronski was.

Wanda didn't have any friends. She came to school alone and went home alone. She always wore a **faded** blue dress that didn't hang right. It was clean, but it looked as though it had never been **iron**ed properly. She didn't have any friends, but a lot of girls talked to her. They waited for her under the **maple** trees on the corner of Oliver Street. Or they **surround**ed her in the

school yard as she stood watching some little girls play hopscotch* on the **worn** hard ground.

"Wanda," Peggy would say in a most **courteous manner**, as though she were talking to Miss Mason or to the **principal** perhaps. "Wanda," she'd say, giving one of her friends a **nudge**, "tell us. How many dresses did you say you had hanging up in your **closet**?"

"A hundred," said Wanda.

"A hundred!" **exclaim**ed all the girls **incredulous**ly, and the little girls would stop playing hopscotch and listen.

"Yeah, a hundred, all lined up," said Wanda. Then her thin lips drew together in silence.

"What are they like? All silk,* I **bet**," said Peggy.

"Yeah, all silk, all colors."

"Velvet,* too?"

"Yeah, velvet, too. A hundred dresses," repeated Wanda **stolid**ly. "All lined up in my closet."

---

* hopscotch 땅에 여러 개의 사각형을 그어 놓고 번호 또는 순서를 매긴 다음, 사각형 속에 돌 멩이 같은 작은 물체를 던져 사각형들 사이를 팔짝팔짝 뛰어 그 물체를 도로 가져오는 놀이.
* silk 비단. 누에고치에서 뽑은 실로 된 섬유로 짠 직물.
* velvet 벨벳. 짧고 부드러운 솜털이 있는 원단.

Then they'd let her go. And then before she'd gone very far, they couldn't help **burst**ing **into shriek**s and **peal**s of **laughter**.

A hundred dresses! **Obvious**ly the only dress Wanda had was the blue one she wore every day. So what did she say she had a hundred for? What a story!* And the girls laughed **derisively**, while Wanda moved over to the sunny place by the **ivy**-covered **brick** wall of the school building where she usually stood and waited for the bell to ring.

But if the girls had met her at the corner of Oliver Street, they'd carry her along with them for a way, stopping every few feet* for more incredulous questions. And it wasn't always dresses they talked about. Sometimes it was hats, or coats, or even shoes.

"How many shoes did you say you had?"

"Sixty."

"Sixty! Sixty pairs or sixty shoes?"

★ what a story 말도 안 돼! 거짓말이야!
⚡ feet 길이 단위 피트. 1피트는 약 12인치 또는 30.48센티미터이다.

"Sixty pairs. All lined up in my closet."

"Yesterday you said fifty."

"Now I got sixty."

Cries of **exaggerated politeness greet**ed this.

"All alike?" said the girls.

"Oh, no. Every pair is different. All colors. All lined up." And Wanda would **shift** her eyes quickly from Peggy to a **distant spot**, as though she were looking far ahead, looking but not seeing anything.

Then the **outer fringe** of the crowd of girls would **break away gradual**ly, laughing, and little by little, in pairs, the group would **disperse**. Peggy, who had thought up this game, and Maddie, her **inseparable** friend, were always the last to leave. And finally Wanda would move up the street, her eyes **dull** and her mouth closed tight, **hitch**ing her left shoulder **every now and then** in the funny way she had, finishing the walk to school alone.

Peggy was not really **cruel**. She protected small children from **bullies**. And she cried for hours if she saw an animal **mistreat**ed. If anybody had said to her, "Don't you think that is a cruel way to treat Wanda?" she would have been very surprised. Cruel? What did the girl want to go and say she had a hundred dresses for? Anybody could tell that was a lie. Why did she want to lie? And she wasn't just an **ordinary** person, else why would she have a name like that? Anyway, they never made her cry.

As for Maddie, this business of asking Wanda every day how many dresses and how many hats and how many this and that she had was **bother**ing her. Maddie was poor herself. She usually wore somebody's **hand-me-down** clothes. Thank **goodness** she didn't live up on Boggins Heights or have a funny name. And her **forehead** didn't shine the way Wanda's round one did. What did she use on it? Sapolio?* That's what all the girls wanted to know.

Sometimes when Peggy was asking Wanda those questions in that **mock** polite voice, Maddie felt **embarrass**ed and studied the **marble**s in the **palm** of her hand, rolling them around and saying nothing herself. Not that she felt sorry for Wanda **exact**ly. She would never have paid any **attention** to Wanda if Peggy hadn't **invent**ed the dresses game. But

---

★ sapolio 비누 브랜드의 이름.

suppose Peggy and all the others started in on her next! She wasn't as poor as Wanda perhaps, but she was poor. Of course she would have more **sense** than to say a hundred dresses. Still she would not like them to begin on her. Not at all! Oh, dear! She did wish Peggy would stop **teasing** Wanda Petronski.

A BRIGHT BLUE DAY

SOMEHOW Maddie could not **buckle** down to work.

She **sharpen**ed her pencil, turning it around carefully in the little red sharpener, letting the **shavings** fall in a **neat heap** on a piece of **scrap** paper, and trying not to get any of the **dust** from the **lead** on her clean **arithmetic** paper.

A **slight frown puckered** her **forehead. In the first place** she didn't like being late to school. And in the second place she kept thinking about Wanda. Somehow Wanda's desk, though empty, seemed to be the only thing she saw when she looked over to that side of the room.

How had the hundred dresses game begun in the first place? she asked herself **impatient**ly. It was hard to remember the time when they hadn't played that game with Wanda; hard to think all the way back from now, when the hundred dresses was like the daily dozen,* to then, when everything seemed much nicer. Oh, yes. She remembered. It had begun that day when Cecile first wore her new red dress. Suddenly the whole **scene flash**ed **swift**ly and **vivid**ly before Maddie's eyes.

It was a bright blue day in September. No, it must, have been October, because when she and Peggy were coming to school, arms around each other and singing,

---

★ **daily dozen** 일과로 하는 임무. 건강을 위해 매일 하는 12종류의 체조를 가리키는 말에서 유래했다.

Peggy had said, "You know what? This must be the kind of day they mean when they say, 'October's bright blue weather.'"

Maddie remembered that because **afterwards** it didn't seem like bright blue weather anymore, although the weather had not changed in the slightest.

As they turned from **shady** Oliver Street into Maple, they both **blinked**. For now the morning sun shone straight in their eyes. **Besides** that, bright flashes of color came from a group of a half **dozen** or more girls across the street. Their sweaters and jackets and dresses, blues and golds and reds, and one **crimson** one in **particular,** caught the sun's **rays** like bright pieces of glass.

A **crisp**, fresh wind was blowing, **swish**ing their skirts and blowing their hair in their eyes. The girls were all **exclaim**ing and shouting and each one was trying to talk louder than the others. Maddie and Peggy joined the group, and the laughing, and the talking.

"Hi, Peg! Hi, Maddie!" they were **greet**ed warmly. "Look at Cecile!"

What they were all exclaiming about was the dress that Cecile had on—a crimson dress with cap and socks to match. It was a bright new dress and very pretty. Everyone was **admiring** it and admiring Cecile. For long, **slender** Cecile was a **toe** dancer* and wore **fancier** clothes than most of them. And she had her black satin* bag with her **precious** white satin ballet slippers* **slung** over her shoulders. Today was the day for her dancing lesson.

★ toe dance 발레 등에서 발끝으로 추는 춤. 이 기법을 위하여 토슈즈가 쓰인다.
✳ satin 공단. 표면이 매끄럽고 광택이 있는 섬유.
✴ ballet slippers 발레를 할 때 신는 신발.

Maddie sat down on the granite* curbstone* to tie her **shoelaces**. She listened happily to what they were saying. They all seemed especially **jolly** today, probably because it was such a bright day. Everything **sparkled**. Way down at the end of the street the sun **shimmer**ed and turned to silver the blue water of the **bay**. Maddie picked up a piece of broken mirror and flashed a small circle of light **edge**d with rainbow colors onto the houses, the trees, and the top of the telegraph **pole**.*

And it was then that Wanda had come along with her brother Jake.

They didn't often come to school together. Jake had to get to school very early because he helped old Mr. Heany, the school **janitor**, with the **furnace**, or **raking** up the dry leaves, or other **odd** jobs before school opened. Today he must be late.

Even Wanda looked pretty in this sunshine, and her

★ granite 화강암. 구조용, 장식용 등 건축, 토목용으로 널리 사용된다.
✳ curbstone 연석. 도로의 보도 가장자리를 따라 차도와의 경계를 이루는 돌.
✳ telegraph pole (= telephone pole) 전신주.

pale blue dress looked like a piece of the sky in summer; and that old gray toboggan cap* she wore—it must be something Jake had found—looked almost **jaunty**. Maddie watched them **absentminded**ly as she flashed her piece of broken mirror here and there. And only absentmindedly she noticed Wanda **stop short** when they reached the crowd of laughing and shouting girls.

"Come on," Maddie heard Jake say. "I gotta hurry. I gotta get the doors open and ring the bell."

"You go the rest of the way," said Wanda. "I want to stay here."

Jake **shrug**ged and went on up Maple Street. Wanda slowly approached the group of girls. With each step **forward**, before she put her foot down she seemed to **hesitate** for a long, long time. She approached the group as

---

★ toboggan cap 스타킹과 비슷한 모양의 모자로 끝이 뾰족하다. 니트로 만들어지고 본래 터보건 썰매용으로 사용되었다.

a **timid** animal might, ready to run if anything **alarm**ed it.

Even so, Wanda's mouth was **twisted** into the **vague**st **suggest**ion of a smile. She must feel happy, too, because everybody must feel happy on such a day.

As Wanda joined the outside **fringe** of girls, Maddie stood up, too, and went over close to Peggy to get a good look at Cecile's new dress herself. She forgot about Wanda, and more girls kept coming up, **enlarging** the group and all exclaiming about Cecile's new dress.

"Isn't it lovely!" said one.

"Yeah, I have a new blue dress, but it's not as pretty as that," said another.

"My mother just bought me a **plaid**, one of the Stuart plaids.*"

"I got a new dress for dancing school."

"I'm gonna make my mother get me one just like Cecile's."

Everyone was talking to everybody else. Nobody said

★ Stuart plaids 격자무늬는 원래 스코틀랜드 고원지방에서 각 씨족들이 집안을 상징하기 위해 망토 등에 넣어 사용하던 것으로 그 색과 무늬가 각기 다르다. 스튜어트 플레드는 가장 유명한 격자무늬 가운데 하나이다.

anything to Wanda, but there she was, a part of the crowd. The girls closed in a tighter circle around Cecile, still talking all **at once** and admiring her, and Wanda was somehow **envelop**ed in the group. Nobody talked to Wanda, but nobody even thought about her being there.

Maybe, thought Maddie, remembering what had happened next, maybe she **figure**d all she'd have to do was say something and she'd really be one of the girls. And this would be an easy thing to do because all they were doing was talking about dresses.

Maddie was standing next to Peggy. Wanda was standing next to Peggy on the other side. **All of a sudden**, Wanda **impulsive**ly touched Peggy's arm and said something. Her light blue eyes were shining and she looked excited like the rest of the girls.

"What?" asked Peggy. For Wanda had spoken very softly.

Wanda hesitated a moment and then she repeated her words **firm**ly.

"I got a hundred dresses home."

"That's what I thought you said. A hundred dresses.
A hundred!" Peggy's voice raised itself higher and higher.

"Hey, kids!" she **yelled**. "This girl's got a hundred
dresses."

Silence greeted this, and the crowd which had centered
around Cecile and her new **finery** now centered **curiously**
around Wanda and Peggy. The girls eyed Wanda, first

incredulously, then **suspiciously**.

"A hundred dresses?" they said. "Nobody could have a hundred dresses."

"I have though."

"Wanda has a hundred dresses."

"Where are they then?"

"In my **closet**."

"Oh, you don't wear them to school."

"No. For parties."

"Oh, you mean you don't have any everyday dresses."

"Yes, I have all kinds of dresses."

"Why don't you wear them to school?"

For a moment Wanda was silent to this. Her lips drew together. Then she repeated **stolid**ly as though it were a lesson learned in school, "A hundred of them. All lined up in my closet."

"Oh, I see," said Peggy, talking like a **grown-up** person. "The child has a hundred dresses, but she wouldn't wear them to school. Perhaps she's worried of getting ink or **chalk** on them."

With this everybody fell to laughing and talking at once. Wanda looked stolidly at them, **pursing** her lips together, **wrinkling** her forehead up so that the gray toboggan **slip**ped way down on her brow. Suddenly from down the street the school **gong** rang its first **warn**ing.

"Oh, come on, hurry," said Maddie, **relieved**. "We'll be late."

"Good-bye, Wanda," said Peggy. "Your hundred dresses sound bee-you-tiful."

More shouts of **laughter** greeted this, and off the girls ran, laughing and talking and forgetting Wanda and her hundred dresses. Forgetting until tomorrow and the next day and the next, when Peggy, seeing her coming to school, would remember and ask her about the hundred dresses. For now Peggy seemed to think a day was lost if she had not had some fun with Wanda, winning the

approving laughter of the girls.

Yes, that was the way it had all begun, the game of the hundred dresses. It all happened so suddenly and **unexpected**ly, with everybody falling right in, that even if you felt uncomfortable as Maddie had there wasn't anything you could do about it. Maddie **wag**ged her head up and down. Yes, she repeated to herself, that was the way it began, that day, that bright blue day.

And she **wrap**ped up her shavings and went to the front of the room to empty them in the teacher's basket.

THE CONTEST

Now today, even though she and Peggy had been late
to school, Maddie was glad she had not had to **make
fun of** Wanda. She worked her **arithmetic** problems
absentmindedly. Eight times eight . . . let's see . . . nothing

she could do about making fun of Wanda. She wished she had the **nerve** to write Peggy a note, because she knew she'd never have the **courage** to **speak** right **out** to Peggy, to say, "Hey, Peg, let's stop asking Wanda how many dresses she has."

When she finished her arithmetic, she did start a note to Peggy. Suddenly she **paused** and **shuddered**. She **pictured** herself in the school **yard**, a new target for Peggy and the girls. Peggy might ask her where she got the dress she had on, and Maddie would have to say that it was one of Peggy's old ones that Maddie's mother had tried to **disguise** with new **trim**mings so that no one in Room 13 would **recognize** it.

If only Peggy would decide **of her own accord** to stop having fun with Wanda. Oh, well! Maddie ran her hand through her short **blond** hair as though to push the uncomfortable thoughts away. What difference did it make? Slowly Maddie **tore** the note she had started into **bit**s. She was Peggy's best friend, and Peggy was the best-liked girl in the whole room. Peggy could not possibly do anything that was really wrong, she thought.

As for Wanda, she was just some girl who lived up on Boggins Heights and stood alone in the school yard. Nobody in the room thought about Wanda at all **except** when it was her turn to stand up for **oral** reading. Then they all hoped she would hurry up and finish and sit down, because it took her forever to read a **paragraph**. Sometimes she stood up and just looked at her book and couldn't, or wouldn't, read at all. The teacher tried to help her, but she'd just stand there until the teacher told her to sit down. Was she **dumb** or what? Maybe she was just **timid**. The only time she talked was in the school yard about her hundred dresses. Maddie remembered her telling about one of her dresses, a **pale** blue one with cerise-colored* trimmings. And she remembered another that was **brilliant** jungle green* with a red sash.* "You'd look like a Christmas tree in that," the girls had said in

---

★ cerise 엷은 홍색을 띤 흰색. 프랑스어로 '체리'라는 뜻이다.
✳ jungle green 밀림 속과 같은 어두운 녹색.
✳ sash 장식용으로 허리에 감는 폭넓은 띠.

pretended **admiration**.

Thinking about Wanda and her hundred dresses all lined up in the closet, Maddie began to wonder who was going to win the drawing and color **contest**. For girls, this contest **consist**ed of designing dresses, and for boys, of designing motorboats.* Probably Peggy would win the girls' medal. Peggy drew better than anyone else in the room. At least that's what everybody thought. You should see the way she could copy a picture in a magazine or some film star's head. You could almost tell who it was. Oh, Maddie did hope Peggy would win. Hope so? She was sure Peggy would win. Well, tomorrow the teacher was going to **announce** the winners. Then they'd know.

Thoughts of Wanda **sank** further and further from Maddie's mind, and by the time the history lesson began she had forgotten all about her.

★ motorboat 모터보트. 내연기관으로 추진되는 소형 선박.

THE HUNDRED DRESSES

THE next day it was **drizzling**. Maddie and Peggy hurried to school under Peggy's umbrella. **Naturally** on a day like this they didn't wait for Wanda Petronski on the corner of Oliver Street, the street that far, far away, under the **railroad tracks** and up the hill, led to Boggins **Heights**. Anyway they weren't **taking chances** on being late today, because today was important.

"Do you think Miss Mason will surely **announce** the winners today?" asked Peggy.

"Oh, I hope so, the minute we get in," said Maddie, and added, "Of course you'll win, Peg."

"Hope so," said Peggy **eagerly**.

The minute they entered the classroom they stopped short and **gasped**. There were drawings all over the room, on every **ledge** and **windowsill, tack**ed to the tops of the **blackboard**s, **spread** over the bird charts, **dazzling** colors and **brilliant lavish** designs, all drawn on great **sheet**s of **wrap**ping paper.

There must have been a hundred of them all lined up!

These must be the drawings for the **contest**. They were! Everybody stopped and **whistle**d or **murmur**ed **admiring**ly.

As soon as the class had **assembled** Miss Mason announced the winners. Jack Beggles had won for the boys, she said,

and his design of an outboard motorboat* was on **exhibition** in Room 12, along with the sketches by all the other boys.

"As for the girls," she said, "although just one or two sketches were **submit**ted by most, one girl—and Room 13 should be very proud of her—this one girl actually drew one hundred designs—all different and all beautiful. In the **opinion** of the **judge**s, any one of her drawings is **worthy** of winning the prize. I am happy to say that Wanda Petronski is the winner of the girls' medal. **Unfortunately** Wanda has been **absent** from school for some days and is not here to receive the **applause** that is **due** her. Let us hope she will be back tomorrow. Now, class, you may **file** around the room quietly and look at her **exquisite** drawings."

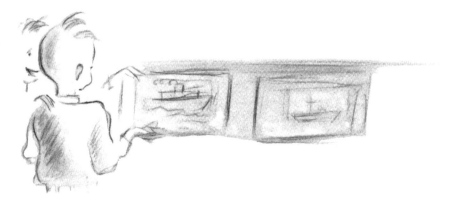

The children **burst into** applause, and even the boys were glad to have a chance to **stamp** on the floor, put their fingers in their mouths and whistle, though they were not interested in dresses. Maddie and Peggy were among the first to reach the blackboard to look at the drawings.

"Look, Peg," **whisper**ed Maddie, "there's that blue one she told us about. Isn't it beautiful?"

"Yeah," said Peggy, "and here's that green one. Boy,* and I thought I could draw!"

While the class was circling the room, the **monitor** from the **principal**'s office brought Miss Mason a note. Miss

---

✷ outboard motorboat 아웃보드 엔진이 있는 유람선. 내륙의 수로에서 유람과 수상 스키를 즐길 수 있다.
✷ boy 어머나! 맙소사! '소년'이라는 뜻의 명사가 아니라 놀람 · 기쁨 · 아픔 등을 나타내는 감탄사로 쓰였다.

Mason read it several times and studied it **thoughtful**ly for
a while. Then she **clap**ped her hands and said, "**Attention**,
class. Everyone back to his seat."

When the **shuffling** of feet had stopped and the room
was still and quiet, Miss Mason said, "I have a letter from
Wanda's father that I want to read to you."

★ Polack 폴란드인 혹은 폴란드계 사람을 모욕적으로 말하는 표현.
✳ yours truly 격식을 차리는 편지의 마무리 말.

Miss Mason stood there a moment and the silence in the room grew **tense** and **expectant**. The teacher **adjust**ed her glasses slowly and **deliberately**. Her **manner indicate**d that what was coming—this letter from Wanda's father —was a matter of great importance. Everybody listened closely as Miss Mason read the **brief** note:

"Dear teacher: My Wanda will not come to your school anymore. Jake also. Now we move away to big city. No more **holler** Polack.* No more ask why funny name. Plenty of funny names in the big city.

Yours truly,* Jan Petronski."

A deep silence met the reading of this letter. Miss Mason took her glasses off, blew on them, and **wiped** them on her soft white **handkerchief**. Then she put them on again and looked at the class. When she spoke her voice was very low.

"I am sure none of my boys and girls in Room 13 would **purposely** and deliberately hurt anyone's feelings because his name happened to be a long, **unfamiliar** one. I **prefer** to think that what was said was said in **thoughtless**ness. I know that all of you feel the way I do, that this is a very unfortunate thing to have happen. Unfortunate and sad, both. And I want you all to think about it."

The first **period** was a study period.* Maddie tried to prepare her lessons, but she could not **put her mind on** her work. She had a very sick feeling in the bottom of her **stomach**. True, she had not enjoyed listening to Peggy ask Wanda how many dresses she had in her **closet**, but she had said nothing. She had **stood by** silently, and that

---

★ study period 수업이 없는 자습 시간.

was just as bad as what Peggy had done. Worse. She was a **coward**. At least Peggy hadn't considered they were being **mean**, but she, Maddie, had thought they were doing wrong. She had thought, supposing she was the one being **made fun of**. She could **put herself in Wanda's shoes**. But she had done just as much as Peggy to make life **miserable** for Wanda by simply standing by and saying nothing. She had helped to make someone so unhappy that she had had to move away from town.

Goodness! Wasn't there anything she could do? If only she could tell Wanda she hadn't meant to hurt her feelings. She turned around and **stole** a **glance** at Peggy,

but Peggy did not look up. She seemed to be studying hard.

Well, whether Peggy felt badly or not, she, Maddie, had to do something. She had to find Wanda Petronski. Maybe she had not yet moved away. Maybe Peggy would climb the Heights with her and they would tell Wanda she had won the contest. And that they thought she was smart and the hundred dresses were beautiful.

When school was **dismiss**ed in the afternoon, Peggy said with **pretend**ed **casual**ness, "Hey, let's go and see if that kid has left town or not."

So Peggy had had the same idea as Maddie had had! Maddie **glow**ed. Peggy was really all right, just as she always thought. Peg was really all right. She was okay.

UP ON BOGGINS HEIGHTS

THE two girls hurried out of the building, up the street toward Boggins **Height**s, the part of town that wore such a **forbidding** air on this kind of November afternoon, **drizzly**, **damp**, and **dismal**.

"Well, at least," said Peggy **gruff**ly, "I never did call her a **foreigner** or **make fun of** her name. I never thought she had the **sense** to know we were making fun of her anyway. I thought she was too **dumb**. And, gee,* look how she can draw! And I thought I could draw."

Maddie could say nothing. All she hoped was that they would find Wanda. Just so she'd be able to tell her they were sorry they had all **picked on** her. And just to say how wonderful the whole school thought she was, and please not to move away and everybody would be nice. She and Peggy would fight anybody who was not nice.

Maddie fell to imagining a story in which she and Peggy **assail**ed any **bully** who might be going to pick on Wanda. "Petronski—Onski!" somebody would **yell**, and she and Peggy would **pounce** on the **guilty** one. For a time Maddie **console**d herself with these thoughts, but they soon **vanish**ed and again she felt unhappy and wished everything could be nice the way it was before any of them had made fun of Wanda.

★ gee 야! 와! 놀람과 감탄을 나타내는 감탄사.

Br-r-r! How **drab** and cold and **cheerless** it was up here on the Heights! In the summertime the woods, the **sumac**, and the **ferns** that grew along the **brook** on the side of the road were **lush** and made this a beautiful walk on Sunday afternoons. But now it did not seem beautiful. The brook had **shrunk** to the **merest trickle**, and today's drizzle **sharpen**ed the **outlines** of the **rusty tin** cans, old shoes, and **forlorn remnant**s of a big black umbrella in the **bed** of the brook.

The two girls hurried on. They hoped to get to the top of the hill before dark. **Otherwise** they were not certain they could find Wanda's house. At last, **puff**ing and **pant**ing, they **round**ed the top of the hill. The first house, that old **rickety** one, belonged to old man Svenson. Peggy and Maddie hurried past it almost on **tiptoe**. Somebody said once that old man Svenson had shot a man. Others said, "**Nonsense!** He's an old good-for-nothing.* Wouldn't hurt a **flea**."

★ good-for-nothing 아무 짝에도 쓸모 없는 사람을 말하는 표현.

But, false or not, the girls breathed more freely as they rounded the corner. It was too cold and drizzly for old man Svenson to be in his **customary** chair **tilt**ed against the house, chewing and **spit**ting tobacco juice.★ Even his dog was nowhere in **sight** and had not **bark**ed at the girls from wherever he might be.

"I think that's where the Petronkis live," said Maddie, pointing to a little white house with lots of chicken **coop**s at the side of it. **Wisp**s of old grass **stuck** up here and there along the **pathway** like thin wet **kittens**. The house and its **sparse** little **yard** looked **shabby** but clean. It reminded Maddie of Wanda's one dress, her **faded** blue cotton dress, shabby but clean.

There was not a sign of life about the house **except** for a yellow cat, half grown, **crouch**ing on the one small

---

★ tobacco juice 담배 때문에 갈색으로 변한 침.

step close to the front door. It **leapt timid**ly with a
small cry **halfway** up a tree when the girls came into
the yard. Peggy **knock**ed **firm**ly on the door, but
there was no answer. She and Maddie went around
to the **backyard** and knocked there. Still there was
no answer.

"Wanda!" called Peggy. They listened sharply,
but only a deep silence pressed against their **eardrum**s.
There was no doubt about it. The Petronskis were
gone.

"Maybe they just went away for a little while and
haven't really left with their **furniture** yet," **suggest**ed
Maddie **hopeful**ly. Maddie was beginning to wonder
how she could **bear** the **hard fact** that Wanda had

actually gone and that she might never be able to make **amend**s.

"Well," said Peggy, "let's see if the door is open."

They **cautious**ly turned the **knob** of the front door. It opened easily, for it was a light thing and looked as though it **furnish**ed but **frail** protection against the cold winds that blew up here in the wintertime. The little square room that the door opened into was empty. There was **absolute**ly nothing left in it, and in the corner a closet with its door wide open was empty, too. Maddie wondered what it had held before the Petronskis moved out. And she thought of Wanda saying, "Sure, a hundred dresses . . . all lined up in the closet."

Well, anyway, real and **imaginary** dresses alike were gone. The Petronskis were gone. And now how could she and Peggy tell Wanda anything? Maybe the teacher knew where she had moved to. Maybe old man Svenson knew. They might knock on his door and ask on the way down. Or the post office might know. If they wrote a letter, Wanda might get it because the post office might **forward** it. Feeling very **downcast** and **discouraged**, the

girls closed the door and started for home. Coming down the road, way, way off in the **distance**, through the drizzle they could see the water of the **bay**, gray and cold.

"Do you suppose that was their cat and they forgot her?" asked Peggy. But the cat wasn't anywhere around now, and as the girls turned the **bend** they saw her crouching under the **dilapidated** wooden chair in front of old man Svenson's house. So perhaps the cat belonged to him. They lost their **courage** about knocking on his door and asking when the Petronskis had left and anyway, **goodness!** here was old man Svenson himself coming up the road. Everything about Svenson was yellow; his house, his cat, his **trousers**, his **drooping mustache** and **tangled** hair, his **hound loping** behind him, and the long **streams** of tobacco juice he **expert**ly shot from between his **scatter**ed yellow teeth. The two girls drew over to the side of the **path** as they hurried by. When they were a good way past, they stopped.

"Hey, Mr. Svenson!" yelled Peggy. "When did the Petronskis move?"

Old man Svenson turned around, but said nothing.
Finally he did answer, but his words were un**intelligible**,
and the two girls turned and ran down the hill as fast
as they could. Old man Svenson looked after them for
a moment and then went on up the hill, **mutter**ing to
himself and **scratch**ing his head.

When they were back down on Oliver Street again,
the girls stopped running. They still felt **disconsolate**, and

Maddie wondered if she were going to be unhappy about Wanda and the hundred dresses forever. Nothing would ever seem good to her again, because just when she was about to enjoy something—like going for a hike with Peggy to look for bayberries* or **sliding** down Barley Hill —she'd **bump** right **smack** into the thought that she had

---

* bayberry 월계수 열매. 타원처럼 생긴 공 모양으로, 10월에 검은 빛을 띤 자주색으로 익는다.

made Wanda Petronski move away.

"Well, anyway," said Peggy, "she's gone now, so what can we do? **Besides**, when I was asking her about all of her dresses she probably was getting good ideas for her drawings. She might not even have won the contest otherwise."

Maddie carefully **turn**ed this idea **over** in her head, for if there were anything in it she would not have to feel so bad. But that night she could not get to sleep. She thought about Wanda and her faded blue dress and the little house she had lived in; and old man Svenson living a few steps away. And she thought of the **glow**ing picture those hundred dresses made—all lined up in the classroom.

At last Maddie sat up in bed and pressed her **forehead** tight in her hands and really thought. This was the hardest thinking she had ever done. After a long, long time she reached an important **conclusion**.

She was never going to **stand by** and say nothing again.

If she ever heard anybody picking on someone because they were funny looking or because they had strange

names, she'd **speak up**. Even if it meant losing Peggy's **friendship**. She had no way of making things right with Wanda, but from now on she would never make anybody else so unhappy again. Finally, all tired out, Maddie fell asleep.

THE LETTER TO ROOM 13

ON Saturday Maddie spent the afternoon with Peggy. They were writing a letter to Wanda Petronski.

It was just a **friendly** letter telling about the **contest** and telling Wanda she had won. They told her how pretty her drawings were, and that now they were studying about Winfield Scott* in school. And they asked her if she liked where she was living now and if she liked her new teacher. They had meant to say they were sorry, but it ended up with their just writing a friendly letter, the kind they would have written to any good friend, and they signed it with lots of X's* for love.

They mailed the letter to Boggins Heights, writing "Please **Forward**" on the **envelope**. The teacher had not known where Wanda had moved to, so their only hope was that the post office knew. The minute they dropped the letter in the **mailbox** they both felt happier and more **carefree**.

Days passed and there was no answer, but the letter did not come back so maybe Wanda had received it. Perhaps she was so hurt and angry she was not going to answer. You could not **blame** her. And Maddie remembered the way she **hitch**ed her left shoulder up as she walked off to school alone, and how the girls always said, "Why does

---

★ Winfield Scott 윈필드 스콧. 미국의 군인으로, 대영 전쟁 때 퀸스타운헤이츠 전투, 치퍼와 전투, 런디즈레인 전투에 참가했다.
＊X 편지 말미 등에 붙이는 키스 표시.

her dress always hang funny like that, and why does she wear those **queer**, high, **lace**d shoes?"

They knew she didn't have any mother, but they hadn't thought about it. They hadn't thought she had to do her own washing and **iron**ing. She only had one dress and she must have had to wash and iron it **overnight**. Maybe sometimes it wasn't dry when it was time to put it on in the morning. But it was always clean.

Several weeks went by and still Wanda did not answer. Peggy had begun to forget the whole business, and Maddie put herself to sleep at night making speeches about Wanda, defending her from great crowds of girls who were trying to **tease** her with, "How many dresses have you got?" Before Wanda could press her lips together in a tight line the way she did before answering, Maddie would cry out, "Stop! This girl is just a girl just like you are . . ." And then everybody would feel **ashamed** the way she used to feel. Sometimes she **rescue**d Wanda from a **sink**ing ship or the **hoof**s of a **runaway** horse. "Oh, that's all right," she'd say when Wanda thanked her with **dull pained** eyes.

Now it was Christmastime and there was snow on the ground. Christmas bells and a small tree **decorate**d the classroom. And on one narrow **blackboard** Jack Beggles had drawn a **jolly** fat Santa Claus in red and white **chalk**. On the last day of school before the holidays, the children in Peggy and Maddie's class had a Christmas party. The teacher's desk was rolled back and a piano rolled in. First the children had acted the story of Tiny Tim.* Then they had sung songs and Cecile had done some dances in different **costume**s. The dance called the "Passing of

Autumn," in which she **whirl**ed and **spun** like a red and golden autumn leaf, was the favorite.

After the party the teacher said she had a surprise,

★ Tiny Tim 찰스 디킨즈의 소설 '크리스마스 캐럴'에 등장하는 Timothy Cratchit라는 캐릭터의 별명이다. 잠깐 등장하는 조연이지만 주인공의 선택에 대한 결과를 상징하는 중요한 인물이다.

and she showed the class a letter she had received that morning.

"Guess who this is from," she said. "You remember Wanda Petronski? The bright little artist who won the drawing contest? Well, she has written me and I am glad to know where she lives because now I can send her medal. And I hope it gets there for Christmas. I want to read her letter to you."

The class sat up with a sudden interest, and listened **intent**ly to Miss Mason as she read the letter.

"Dear Miss Mason:

How are you and Room 13? Please tell the girls they can keep those hundred dresses because in my new house I have a hundred new ones all lined up in my **closet**. I'd like that girl Peggy to have the drawing of the green dress with the red **trim**ming and her friend Maddie to have the blue one. For Christmas. I miss that school and my new teacher does not **equalize** with you. Merry Christmas to you and everybody.

Yours truly, Wanda Petronski."

The teacher passed the letter around the room for everybody to see. It was pretty, decorated with a picture of a Christmas tree lighted up in the night in a park **surround**ed by high buildings.

On the way home from school Maddie and Peggy held their drawings very carefully. They had stayed late to help **straighten** up after the play and it was getting dark. The houses looked warm and inviting with wreaths*

★ wreath 리스. 크리스마스 때 문에 장식으로 거는 동그란 모양의 화환.

and holly* and lighted trees in their windows. Outside the **grocery** store hundreds of Christmas trees were **stack**ed, and in the window candy peppermint **canes*** and **cornucopias*** of shiny bright **transparent** paper were **strung**. The air smelled like Christmas and bright lights everywhere **reflect**ed different colors on the snow.

"The colors are like the colors in Wanda's hundred dresses," said Maddie.

"Yes," said Peggy, holding her drawing out to look at it under the street lamp. "And boy! This shows she really liked us. It shows she got our letter and this is her way of saying that everything's all right. And **that's that**," she said with **finality**.

Peggy felt happy and **relieved**. It was Christmas and everything was fine.

"I hope so," said Maddie sadly. She felt sad because

★ holly 호랑가시나무. 잎가에 뾰족뾰족한 가시가 돋아 있고 새빨간 열매가 달리는 나무로 크리스마스 때 장식용으로 쓰인다.
✳ candy cane 크리스마스에 먹는 지팡이 모양 사탕.
❋ cornucopia 풍요를 상징하는 원뿔 모양의 장식물.

she knew she would never see the little **tight-lipped** Polish girl again and couldn't ever really make things right between them.

She went home and she **pin**ned her drawing over a **torn** place in the pink-flowered wallpaper in the bedroom. The **shabby** room **came alive** from the **brilliancy** of the colors. Maddie sat down on the **edge** of her bed and looked at the drawing. She had **stood by** and said nothing, but Wanda had been nice to her anyway.

Tears **blur**red her eyes and she **gazed** for a long time at the picture. Then **hastily** she **rub**bed her eyes and studied it intently. The colors in the dress were so **vivid** she had **scarcely notice**d the face and head of the drawing. But it looked like her, Maddie! It really did. The same short **blond** hair, blue eyes, and wide straight mouth. Why, it really looked like her own self! Wanda had really drawn this for her. Wanda had drawn her! In excitement she ran over to Peggy's.

"Peg!" she said. "Let me see your picture."

"What's the matter?" asked Peggy as they **clatter**ed up the stairs to her room, where Wanda's drawing was lying **facedown** on the bed. Maddie carefully lifted it up.

"Look! She drew you. That's you!" she **exclaim**ed. And the head and face of this picture did look like the **auburn**-haired Peggy.

"What did I say!" said Peggy. "She must have really

liked us anyway."

"Yes, she must have," agreed Maddie, and she **blink**ed away the tears that came every time she thought of Wanda standing alone in that sunny **spot** in the school **yard** close to the wall, looking **stolid**ly over at the group of laughing girls after she had walked off, after she had said, "Sure, a hundred of them—all lined up . . ."

THE
HUNDRED
DRESSES

THE
HUNDRED
DRESSES

ELEANOR ESTES

Contents

'아동 도서계의 노벨상!' 미국 최고 권위의 아동 문학상

뉴베리 상(Newbery Award)은 미국 도서관 협회에서 해마다 미국 아동 문학 발전에 가장 크게 이바지한 작가에게 수여하는 아동 문학상입니다. 1922년에 시작된이 상은 미국에서 가장 오랜 역사를 지닌 아동 문학상이자, '아동 도서계의 노벨상'이라 불릴 만큼 높은 권위를 자랑하는 상입니다.

뉴베리 상은 그 역사와 권위만큼이나 심사 기준이 까다롭기로 유명한데, 심사단은 책의 주제 의식은 물론 정보의 깊이와 스토리의 정교함, 캐릭터와 문체의 적정성 등을 꼼꼼히 평가하여 수상작을 결정합니다.

그해 최고의 작품으로 선정된 도서에게는 '뉴베리 메달(Newbery Medal)'이라고 부르는 금색 메달을 수여하며, 최종 후보에 올랐던 주목할 만한 작품들에게는 '뉴베리 아너(Newbery Honor)'라는 이름의 은색 마크를 수여합니다.

뉴베리 상을 받은 도서는 미국의 모든 도서관에 비치되어 더 많은 독자들을 만나게 되며, 대부분 수십에서 수백만 부가 판매되는 베스트셀러가 됩니다. 뉴베리상을 수상한 작가는 그만큼 필력과 작품성을 인정받게 되어, 수상 작가의 다른작품들 또한 수상작 못지않게 커다란 주목과 사랑을 받습니다.

왜 뉴베리 수상작인가?
쉬운 어휘로 쓰인 '검증된' 영어원서!

뉴베리 수상작들은 '검증된 원서'로 국내 영어 학습자들에게 큰 사랑을 받고 있습니다. 뉴베리 수상작이 원서 읽기에 좋은 교재인 이유는 무엇일까요?

1. 아동 문학인 만큼 어휘가 어렵지 않습니다.
2. 어렵지 않은 어휘를 사용하면서도 '문학상'을 수상한 만큼 문장의 깊이가 상당합니다.
3. 적당한 난이도의 어휘와 깊이 있는 문장으로 구성되어 있기 때문에 초등 고학년부터 성인까지, 영어 초보자부터 실력자까지 모든 영어 학습자들이 읽기에 좋습니다.

실제로 뉴베리 수상작은 국제중·특목고에서는 입시 필독서로, 대학교에서는 영어 강독 교재로 다양하고 폭넓게 활용되고 있습니다. 이런 이유로 뉴베리 수상작은 한국어 번역서보다 오히려 원서가 훨씬 많이 판매되는 기현상을 보이고 있습니다.

'베스트 오브 베스트'만을 엄선한 「뉴베리 컬렉션」

「뉴베리 컬렉션」은 뉴베리 메달 및 아너 수상작, 그리고 뉴베리 수상 작가의 유명 작품들을 엄선하여 한국 영어 학습자들을 위한 최적의 교재로 재탄생시킨 영어 원서 시리즈입니다.

1. 어휘 수준과 문장의 난이도, 분량 등 국내 영어 학습자들에게 적합한 정도를 종합적으로 검토하여 선정하였습니다.
2. 기존 원서 독자층 사이의 인기도까지 감안하여 최적의 작품들을 선별하였습니다.
3. 판형이 좁고 글씨가 작아 읽기 힘들었던 원서 디자인을 대폭 수정하여, 판형을 시원하게 키우고 읽기에 최적화된 영문 서체를 사용하여 가독성을 극대화하였습니다.
4. 함께 제공되는 워크북은 어려운 어휘를 완벽하게 정리하고 이해력을 점검하는 퀴즈를 덧붙여 독자들이 원서를 보다 쉽고 재미있게 읽을 수 있도록 구성하였습니다.
5. 기존에 높은 가격에 판매되어 구입이 부담스러웠던 오디오북을 부록으로 제공하여 리스닝과 소리 내어 읽기에까지 원서를 두루 활용할 수 있도록 했습니다.

엘레노어 에스테스(Eleanor Estes)는 미국 아동 문학 작가이자 어린이 도서 사서였습니다. 미국 코네티컷 주에서 태어난 에스테스는 오랜 시간 사서로 일하다가 1941년 「The Moffats」를 출간하며 작가로서의 삶을 시작했습니다. 그 후 그녀는 약 20여편의 작품을 썼으며, 그 작품들은 주로 코네티컷 주의 작은 마을에서 살았던 그녀의 경험을 토대로 하고 있습니다. 이러한 그녀의 작품 가운데 가장 잘 알려진 것은 「The Hundred Dresses」로, 자신이 어렸을 때 친구가 입던 옷을 물려받았던 경험과 놀림 받던 다른 친구를 옹호해 주지 못했던 그녀의 죄책감이 담겨 있습니다. 이렇게 자신의 삶을 바탕으로 쓰여진 에스테스의 작품들은 독자들에게 큰 감동을 주어 많은 상을 받았습니다. 루이스 캐롤 상을 받은 「The Moffats」의 후속 작품 두 편 「The Middle Moffat」, 「Rufus M」으로 뉴베리 아너를, 그리고 「The Hundred Dresses」로도 역시 뉴베리 아너를 수상하였고 1954년 「Ginger Pye」로는 뉴베리 메달을 수상하였습니다.

「The Hundred Dresses」는 매일같이 학교에 빛바랜 파란색 드레스를 입고 오는 Wanda에 대한 이야기입니다. 하지만 그녀는 자신의 집 옷장에 백 벌의 아름다운 드레스가 모두 줄지어 걸려 있다고 이야기합니다. 다른 여자아이들은 그 말을 믿지 않고 매일 그녀를 놀립니다. 그리고 어느 날부터 Wanda가 학교에 나오지 않습니다. 학교에서 그림 그리기 대회의 우승자가 발표되던 날 아이들은 Wanda가 말하던 백 벌의 드레스에 대한 진실과 그녀가 학교에 오지 않는 이유에 대해 알게 되자 끔찍한 기분을 느낍니다. 하지만 아이들이 그녀에게 사과를 하기에는 너무 늦어버린 것 같습니다.
세월이 흘러도 변함없는 호소력을 지닌 이 책은 친절함, 동정심, 그리고 올바른 일을 위해서 맞선다는 것의 진정한 의미를 독자들에게 전달하고 있습니다.

원서 본문

내용이 담긴 원서 본문입니다.
원어민이 읽는 일반 원서와 같은 텍스트지만,
암기해야 할 중요 어휘들은 볼드체로 표시되
어 있습니다. 이 어휘들은 지금 들고 계신 워
크북에 챕터별로 정리되어 있습니다.

학습 심리학 연구 결과에 따르면, 한 단어씩
따로 외우는 단어 암기는 거의 효과가 없다고
합니다. 단어를 제대로 외우기 위해서는 문맥
(context) 속에서 단어를 암기해야 하며, 한 단
어당 문맥 속에서 15번 이상 마주칠 때 완벽하
게 암기할 수 있다고 합니다.

이 책의 본문에서는 중요 어휘를 볼드체로 강조하여, 문맥 속의 단어들을 더 확
실히 인지(word cognition in context)하도록 돕고 있습니다. 또한 대부분의 중요 단
어들은 다른 챕터에서도 반복해서 등장하기 때문에 이 책을 읽는 것만으로도 자
연스럽게 어휘력을 향상시킬 수 있습니다.

또한 본문 하단에는 내용 이해를 돕기 위한
'각주'가 첨가되어 있습니다. 각주는 굳이 암기
할 필요는 없지만, 알아 두면 도움이 될 만한
정보를 설명하고 있습니다. 각주를 참고하면
스토리를 더 깊이 있게 이해할 수 있어 원서를
읽는 재미가 배가됩니다.

the Gettysburg Address,* for that was the way Miss
Mason always began the **session**. Peggy and Maddie
slipped into their seats just as the class was saying the
last lines . . .

"that these dead shall not have died in **vain**; that the
nation shall, under God, have a new birth of freedom,
and that **government** of the people, by the people, for
the people, shall not **perish** from the earth."

* Gettysburg Address 게티스버그 연설. 미국 남북 전쟁이 진행되던 1863년 11월 19일, 격
전지였던 펜실베이니아주 게티스버그에서 전사한 장병들의 명복을 위로하는 추도식에서
이루어진 16대 대통령 링컨의 연설.

1. WANDA   9

워크북(Workbook)

Check Your Reading Speed
해당 챕터의 단어 수가 기록되어 있어, 리딩 속도를 측정할 수 있습니다. 특히 리딩 속도를 중시하는 독자들이 유용하게 사용할 수 있습니다.

Build Your Vocabulary
본문에 볼드 표시되어 있던 단어들이 정리되어 있습니다. 리딩 전, 후에 반복해서 보면 원서를 더욱 쉽게 읽을 수 있고, 어휘력도 빠르게 향상 됩니다.

단어는 〈스펠링 – 빈도 – 발음기호 – 품사 – 한글 뜻 – 영문 뜻〉 순서로 표기되어 있으며 빈도 표시(★)가 많을수록 필수 어휘입니다. 반복해서 등장하는 단어는 빈도 대신 '복습'으로 표기되어 있습니다. 품사는 아래와 같이 표기했습니다.

n. 명사 | **a.** 형용사 | **ad.** 부사 | **v.** 동사

conj. 접속사 | **prep.** 전치사 | **int.** 감탄사 | **idiom** 숙어 및 관용구

Comprehension Quiz
간단한 퀴즈를 통해 읽은 내용에 대한 이해력을 점검해 볼 수 있습니다.

「뉴베리 컬렉션」 이렇게 읽어 보세요!

아래와 같이 프리뷰(Preview) → 리딩(Reading) → 리뷰(Review) 세 단계를 거치면서 읽으면, 더욱 효과적으로 영어 실력을 향상할 수 있습니다.

1. 프리뷰(Preview) : 오늘 읽을 내용을 먼저 점검하자!

- 워크북을 통해 오늘 읽을 챕터에 나와 있는 단어들을 쭉 훑어봅니다. 어떤 단어들이 나오는지, 내가 아는 단어와 모르는 단어는 어떤 것들이 있는지 가벼운 마음으로 살펴봅니다.
- 평소처럼 하나하나 쓰면서 암기하려고 하지는 마세요! 익숙하지 않은 단어들을 주의 깊게 보되, 어차피 리딩을 하면서 점차 익숙해질 단어라는 것을 기억하며 빠르게 훑어봅니다.
- 뒤 챕터로 갈수록 '복습'이라고 표시된 단어들이 늘어나는 것을 알 수 있습니다. '복습' 단어인데도 여전히 익숙하지 않다면 더욱 신경을 써서 봐야겠죠? 매일매일 꾸준히 읽는다면, 익숙한 단어들이 점점 많아진다는 것을 몸으로 느낄 수 있습니다.

2. 리딩(Reading) : 내용에 집중하며 빠르게 읽어 나가자!

- 프리뷰를 마친 후 바로 리딩을 시작합니다. 방금 살펴봤던 어휘들을 문장 속에서 다시 만나게 되는데, 이 과정에서 단어의 쓰임새와 어감을 자연스럽게 익히게 됩니다.
- 모르는 단어나 이해되지 않는 문장이 나오더라도 멈추지 말고 전체적인 맥락을 파악하면서 속도감 있게 읽어 나가세요. 이해되지 않는 문장들은 따로 표시를 하되, 일단 넘어가고 계속 읽는 것이 좋습니다. 뒷부분을 읽다 보면 자연히 이해가 되는 경우도 있고, 정 이해가 되지 않는 부분은 리딩을 마친 이후에 따로 리뷰하는 시간을 가지면 됩니다. 문제집을 풀듯이 모든 문장을 분석하면서 원서를 읽는 것이 아니라, 리딩을 할 때는 리딩에만, 리뷰를 할 때는 리뷰에만 집중하는 것이 필요합니다.
- 볼드 처리된 단어의 의미가 궁금하더라도 워크북을 바로 펼치지 마세요. 정 궁금하다면 한 번씩 참고하는 것도 나쁘진 않지만, 워크북과 원서를 번갈아 보면서 읽는 것은 리딩의 흐름을 끊고 단어 하나하나에 집착하는 좋지 않은 리딩 습관을 심어 줄 수 있습니다.
- 같은 맥락에서 번역서를 구해 원서와 동시에 번갈아 보는 것도 좋은 방법이 아닙니다. 한글 번역을 가지고 있다고 해도 일단 영어로 읽을 때는 영어에만 집중하고 어느 정도 분량을 읽은 후에 번역서와 비교하도록 하세요. 모든 문장을

일일이 번역해서 완벽하게 이해하려는 것은 오히려 좋지 않은 리딩 습관을 심어 주어 장기적으로는 바람직하지 않은 결과를 얻을 수 있습니다. 처음부터 완벽하게 이해하려고 하는 것보다는 빠른 속도로 2~3회 반복해서 읽는 방식이 실력 향상에 더 도움이 됩니다. 만일 반복해서 읽어도 내용이 전혀 이해되지 않아 곤란하다면 책 선정에 문제가 있다고 할 수 있습니다. 그럴 때는 좀 더 쉬운 책을 골라 실력을 다진 뒤 다시 도전하는 것이 좋습니다.

- 초보자라면 분당 150단어의 리딩 속도를 목표로 잡고 리딩을 합니다. 분당 150단어는 원어민이 말하는 속도로, 영어 학습자들이 리스닝과 스피킹으로 넘어가기 위해 가장 기초적으로 달성해야 하는 단계입니다. 분당 50~80단어 정도의 낮은 리딩 속도를 가지고 있는 경우는 대부분 영어 실력이 부족해서라기보다 '잘못된 리딩 습관'을 가지고 있어서 그렇습니다. 이해력이 조금 떨어진다고 하더라도 분당 150단어까지는 속도에 대한 긴장감을 놓치지 말고 속도감 있게 읽어 나가도록 하세요.

3. 리뷰(Review) : 이해력을 점검하고 꼼꼼하게 다시 살펴보자!

- 해당 챕터의 Comprehension Quiz를 통해 이해력을 점검해 봅니다.
- 오늘 만난 어휘들을 다시 한번 복습합니다. 이때는 읽으면서 중요하다고 생각했던 단어를 연습장에 써 보면서 꼼꼼하게 외우는 것도 좋습니다.
- 이해가 되지 않는다고 표시해 두었던 부분도 주의 깊게 분석해 봅니다. 다시 한번 문장을 꼼꼼히 읽고, 어떤 이유에서 이해가 되지 않았는지 생각해 봅니다. 따로 메모를 남기거나 노트를 작성하는 것도 좋은 방법입니다.
- 사실 꼼꼼히 리뷰하는 것은 매우 고된 과정입니다. 원서를 읽고 리뷰하는 시간을 가지는 것이 영어 실력 향상에 많은 도움이 되기는 하지만, 이 과정을 철저히 지키려다가 원서 읽기의 재미를 반감시키는 것은 바람직하지 않습니다. 그럴 때는 차라리 리뷰를 가볍게 하는 것이 좋을 수 있습니다. '내용에 빠져서 재미있게', 문제집에서는 상상도 못할 '많은 양'을 읽으면서, 매일매일 조금씩 꾸준히 실력을 키워 가는 것이 원서를 활용하는 기본적인 방법이며, 영어 공부의 왕도입니다. 문제집 풀듯이 원서 읽기를 시도하고 접근해서는 실패할 수밖에 없습니다.
- 이런 방식으로 원서를 끝까지 다 읽었다면, 다시 반복해서 읽거나 오디오북을 활용하는 등 다양한 방식으로 원서 읽기를 확장해 나갈 수 있습니다. 이에 대한 자세한 안내가 워크북 말미에 실려 있습니다.

1. How did the students react to Wanda's first day being absent?
   A. Nobody noticed her absence.
   B. Everyone worried that she might be sick.
   C. Maddie missed talking with her before school.
   D. Maddie and Peggy missed playing with her at recess.

2. Why did people think that Wanda sat in the corner of class?
   A. They thought that she was rough and noisy.
   B. They thought that she liked to laugh out loud.
   C. They thought that those with dirty shoes all sat there.
   D. They thought that she made good marks on her report card.

3. Why were Wanda's shoes usually caked in dried mud?
   A. She walked along the river by herself.
   B. She never cleaned her shoes or clothes.
   C. She liked to play outside with all of the children.
   D. She walked all the way from Boggins Heights.

4. Why did Peggy and Maddie finally notice Wanda's absence?

   A. They wanted to borrow a dress from Wanda.

   B. They had waited for Wanda and were late to school.

   C. They had to ask for her help with a homework assignment.

   D. They were late to school because they went to Wanda's house.

5. Why were Peggy and Maddie waiting for Wanda?

   A. They wanted to borrow a dress.

   B. They wanted to have some fun with her.

   C. They wanted to protect her from bullies.

   D. They wanted to see what new dress she would wear.

6. How did Peggy and Maddie know that they were running late?

   A. They had heard the school bell.

   B. They had checked their watches.

   C. They had seen a school bus pass by them.

   D. They had seen a student who was always late to school.

7. How did Miss Mason begin her session?

   A. The class stood up and exercised.

   B. The class sang 'Happy Birthday.'

   C. The class recited the Gettysburg Address.

   D. The class recited the Declaration of Independence.

Check Your Reading Speed

1분에 몇 단어를 읽는지 리딩 속도를 측정해보세요.

$$\frac{606 \text{ words}}{\text{reading time ( ) sec}} \times 60 = (\quad) \text{ WPM}$$

Build Your Vocabulary

notice***
[nóutis]

v. ~을 의식하다, 알다; 주목하다; n. 신경씀, 주목, 알아챔
If you notice something or someone, you become aware of them.

absent**
[ǽbsənt]

a. 결석한; 없는, 부재한; 멍한; v. 결석하다, 불참하다 (absence n. 결석)
Someone's absence from a place is the fact that they are not there.

row*
[rou]

n. 열, 줄; 노 젓기; v. 노를 젓다
A row of things or people is a number of them arranged in a line.

rough**
[rʌf]

a. (행동이) 거친; (표면이) 고르지 않은; 개략적인
You say that people or their actions are rough when they use too much force and not enough care or gentleness.

mark***
[ma:rk]

n. 점수, 평점; 자국, 흔적; v. 표시하다; 자국을 내다
If someone gets good or high marks for doing something, they have done it well. If they get poor or low marks, they have done it badly.

report card
[ripɔ́:rt ka:rd]

n. (학교의) 성적표, 통지표
A report card is an official written account of how well or how badly a student has done during the term or year that has just finished.

scuffle
[skʌfl]

v. 실랑이를 벌이다, 옥신각신하다; n. 실랑이, 옥신각신함
If people scuffle, they fight for a short time in a disorganized way.

roar*
[rɔ:r]

n. 함성; 으르렁거림, 포효; v. 으르렁거리다; 고함치다
A roar is a loud deep sound made by an animal, or by someone's voice.

laughter*
[lǽftər]

n. 웃음, 웃기; 웃음소리
Laughter is the sound of people laughing, for example because they are amused or happy.

dirt**
[də:rt]

n. 흙; 먼지, 때
You can refer to the earth on the ground as dirt, especially when it is dusty.

noisy*
[nɔ́izi]

a. 시끄러운, 떠들썩한
A noisy person or thing makes a lot of loud or unpleasant noise.

contrary**
[kántreri]

a. ~와는 다른, 반대되는; n. 반대되는 것 (on the contrary idiom 그와는 반대로)
You use on the contrary when you have just said or implied that something is not true and are going to say that the opposite is true.

rare**
[rɛər]

a. 드문, 보기 힘든; 진귀한, 희귀한 (rarely ad. 드물게, 좀처럼 ~하지 않는)
If something rarely happens, it does not happen very often.

14

twist **
[twist]

v. 비틀다, 일그러뜨리다; (고개 · 몸 등을) 돌리다; 구부리다;
n. (고개 · 몸 등을) 돌리기
If you twist something, especially a part of your body, it moves into an unusual, uncomfortable, or bent position, for example because of being hit or pushed, or because you are upset.

crook
[kruk]

v. (손가락이나 팔을) 구부리다; n. 사기꾼 (crooked a. 비뚤어진, 구부러진)
A crooked smile is uneven and bigger on one side than the other.

exact ***
[igzǽkt]

a. 정확한, 정밀한 (exactly ad. 정확히, 꼭, 틀림없이)
You use exactly with a question to show that you disapprove of what the person you are talking to is doing or saying.

unless **
[ənlés]

prep. ~하지 않는 한, ~이 아닌 한
You use unless to introduce the only circumstances in which an event you are mentioning will not take place or in which a statement you are making is not true.

height **
[hait]

n. 높은 곳; (사물의) 높이; (사람의) 키
A height is a high position or place above the ground.

cake **
[kéik]

v. 들러붙다, 뭉쳐지다; n. 케이크
If something is caked with mud, blood, or dirt, it is covered with a thick dry layer of it.

apt *
[æpt]

a. 잘 ~하는, ~하는 경향이 있는; 적절한
If someone is apt to do something, they often do it and so it is likely that they will do it again.

noontime
[nú:ntàim]

n. 한낮, 정오; a. 한낮의
Noontime means the middle of the day.

yard **
[ja:rd]

n. (학교의) 운동장; 마당, 뜰; 정원 (school yard n. 학교 운동장)
The school yard is the large open area with a hard surface just outside a school building, where the schoolchildren can play and do other activities.

except ***
[iksépt]

prep. (누구 · 무엇을) 제외하고는
You use except to introduce the only thing or person that a statement does not apply to, or a fact that prevents a statement from being completely true.

entertain *
[èntərtéin]

v. 즐겁게 해 주다; (집에서 손님을) 접대하다 (entertainment n. 오락(물), 여흥)
If a performer, performance, or activity entertains you, it amuses you, interests you, or gives you pleasure.

track **
[træk]

v. 발자국을 남기다; 추적하다; (자취 등을 따라) 뒤쫓다; n. 길; 자국; (기차) 선로
If you track in something, you leave behind a track of something such as mud or dirt when you walk.

auburn
[ɔ́:bərn]

a. 적갈색의, 황갈색의; n. (머리털 등의) 적갈색, 황갈색
Auburn hair is reddish brown.

curl **
[kə:rl]

v. 곱슬곱슬한 머리카락; v. 곱슬곱슬하다; (둥그렇게) 감다 (curly a. 곱슬곱슬한)
If you have curls, your hair is in the form of tight curves and spirals.

askew
[əskjúː]

a. 삐딱한; ad. 삐딱하게; 경멸하듯이
Something that is askew is not straight or not level with what it should be level with.

precarious
[prikéəriəs]

a. 위태로운, 불안정한
Something that is precarious is not securely held in place and seems likely to fall or collapse at any moment.

tilt*
[tilt]

n. 기울어짐, 젖혀짐; v. 기울다, (뒤로) 젖혀지다; (의견 · 상황 등이) 기울어지다
The tilt of something is the fact that it slopes, or the angle at which it slopes.

slide*
[slaid]

v. 슬며시 움직이다; 미끄러지다; n. 떨어짐; 미끄러짐
If you slide somewhere, you move there smoothly and quietly.

touchdown
[tʌ́tʃdaun]

n. (미식축구에서) 터치다운, 그 득점; (비행기 · 우주선의) 착륙
In rugby and American football, a touchdown is when a team scores points by taking the ball over the opposition's goal line.

race
[reis]

v. 쏜살같이 가다; 경주하다; n. 경주, 달리기 (시합); 경쟁; 인종, 종족
If you race somewhere, you go there as quickly as possible.

recite*
[risáit]

v. 암송하다, 낭독하다; 죽 말하다
When someone recites a poem or other piece of writing, they say it aloud after they have learned it.

unison
[júːnisn]

n. 조화, 화합, 일치 (in unison **idiom** 일제히)
If two or more people do something in unison, they do it together at the same time.

session*
[séʃən]

n. (특정한 활동을 위한) 시간; (의회 등의) 회기; (법정의) 개정
A session of a particular activity is a period of that activity.

slip*
[slip]

v. (들키지 않고) 슬며시 가다, 오다; 미끄러지다; 빠져 나가다; n. (작은) 실수; 미끄러짐
If you slip somewhere, you go there quickly and quietly.

vain*
[vein]

a. 헛된, 소용없는; 자만심이 강한, 허영심이 많은
If you say that something such as someone's death, suffering, or effort was in vain, you mean that it was useless because it did not achieve anything.

nation***
[néiʃən]

n. (한 국가의 전체) 국민; 국가
The nation is sometimes used to refer to all the people who live in a particular country.

government**
[gʌ́vərnmənt]

n. 정부, 정권; 행정, 통치
The government of a country is the group of people who are responsible for governing it.

perish*
[périʃ]

v. 소멸되다; 죽다, 비명횡사하다
If a substance or material perishes, it starts to fall to pieces and becomes useless.

16

chapter two

1. How did Peggy and Maddie feel in a class that had already begun?
   A. They felt like spies.
   B. They felt like teachers.
   C. They felt like intruders.
   D. They felt like good students.

2. How did people feel about Boggins Heights?
   A. They thought that it was close to school.
   B. They thought that it was quiet and peaceful.
   C. They thought that it was a good place to live.
   D. They thought that it was a good place to visit in summer.

3. How did Peggy speak to Wanda about her dresses?
   A. She spoke in a very rude manner.
   B. She spoke in a very loud manner.
   C. She spoke in a very serious manner.
   D. She spoke in a very courteous manner.

4. Why did the girls laugh after Wanda said she had a hundred dresses?
   A. Wanda obviously only had one dress.
   B. They thought that nobody could have a hundred dresses.
   C. Wanda had one hundred dresses but they were all the same.
   D. They thought that it was silly to own so many dresses.

18

5. How did Peggy feel about the way she treated Wanda?
   A. Peggy felt that she was not cruel at all.
   B. Peggy felt that she was being a bully to Wanda.
   C. Peggy felt that Maddie was the one being cruel.
   D. Peggy felt that Wanda had been mean to her first.

6. Which of the following is true about Maddie?
   A. She lived on Boggins Heights.
   B. She usually wore handed-down clothes.
   C. She thought her name was funny.
   D. She had a shiny forehead.

7. Why was Maddie worried about Peggy and the dressses game with Wanda?
   A. She worried that Peggy and the others would make Wanda cry.
   B. She worried that Wanda really did have one hundred dresses.
   C. She worried that Peggy and the others would make fun of her next.
   D. She worried that Wanda would get angry and get them in trouble.

Check Your Reading Speed

1분에 몇 단어를 읽는지 리딩 속도를 측정해보세요.

$$\frac{1,069 \text{ words}}{\text{reading time (}\quad\text{) sec}} \times 60 = (\quad) \text{ WPM}$$

Build Your Vocabulary

intrude*
[intrú:d]

v. 억지로 들이닥치다, 침입하다; 강요하다; 참견하다 (intruder n. 침입자, 불청객)
If someone intrudes into a place, they go there even though they are not allowed to be there.

notice^{복습}
[nóutis]

v. ~을 의식하다, 알다; 주목하다; n. 신경씀, 주목, 알아챔
If you notice something or someone, you become aware of them.

furthermore*
[fə́:rðərmɔ̀:r]

ad. 뿐만 아니라, 더욱이
Furthermore is used to introduce a piece of information or opinion that adds to or supports the previous one.

dust*
[dʌst]

n. (흙)먼지; v. 먼지를 털다 (dusty a. 먼지투성이인)
If places, roads, or other things outside are dusty, they are covered with tiny bits of earth or sand, usually because it has not rained for a long time.

height^{복습}
[hait]

n. 높은 곳; (사물의) 높이; (사람의) 키
A height is a high position or place above the ground.

wildflower
[wáildflàuər]

n. 들꽃, 야생초
Wildflowers are flowers which grow naturally in the countryside, rather than being grown by people in gardens.

hold one's breath

idiom 숨을 멈추다
If you hold your breath, you make yourself stop breathing for a few moments, for example because you are under water.

till***
[təl]

conj. ~(때)까지
If something happens till a particular time, it happens during the period before that time and stops at that time.

yard^{복습}
[ja:rd]

n. 마당, 뜰; (학교의) 운동장; 정원
A yard is a piece of land next to someone's house, with grass and plants growing in it.

disgraceful
[disgréisfəl]

a. 수치스러운, 부끄러운 (disgracefully ad. 망신스럽게도)
If you say that something such as behavior or a situation is disgraceful, you disapprove of it strongly, and feel that the person or people responsible should be ashamed of it.

rusty*
[rʌ́sti]

a. 녹슨, 녹 투성이의; 예전 같지 않은
A rusty metal object such as a car or a machine is covered with rust, which is a brown substance that forms on iron or steel when it comes into contact with water.

20

tin*
[tin]

n. 깡통; 통조림 (tin can n. 빈 깡통)
A tin is a metal container which is filled with food and sealed in order to preserve the food for long periods of time.

strew
[stru:]

v. (strewed–strewn) 흩어지다, 흩뿌려져 있다; 흩뿌리다 (strewn a. 흩어진)
If a place is strewn with things, they are lying scattered there.

straw*
[strɔ:]

n. 짚, 밀짚; 빨대 (straw hat n. 밀짚모자)
Straw consists of the dried, yellowish stalks from crops such as wheat or barley.

no wonder

idiom 당연하다; 놀랄 일이 아니다
If you say 'no wonder,' 'little wonder,' or 'small wonder,' you mean that something is not surprising.

circulate*
[sə́:rkjulèit]

v. (소문 등이) 유포되다; ~을 알리다; 순환하다
If something such as a rumor circulates or is circulated, the people in a place tell it to each other.

scurry
[skə́:ri]

v. 허둥지둥 가다, 종종걸음을 치다; n. 허둥댐
When people or small animals scurry somewhere, they move there quickly and hurriedly, especially because they are frightened.

in broad daylight

idiom 백주 대낮에
If you say that a crime is committed in broad daylight, you are expressing your surprise that it is done during the day when people can see it, rather than at night.

scatter**
[skǽtər]

v. 흩뿌리다; 황급히 흩어지다; n. 소수, 소량 (scattered a. 드문드문 있는)
Scattered things are spread over an area in an untidy or irregular way.

frame**
[freim]

n. (가구 · 건물 등의) 뼈대; (나무 금속 등으로 된) 틀; 액자
(frame house n. (판자를 댄) 목조 가옥)
A frame house is a house that has a timber framework and cladding.

fade*
[feid]

v. (색깔이) 바래다, 희미해지다; 서서히 사라지다, 점점 희미해지다
(faded a. 빛깔이 바랜)
When a colored object fades or when the light fades it, it gradually becomes paler.

iron**
[áiərn]

v. 다리미질을 하다; n. 철, 쇠
If you iron clothes, you remove the creases from them using an iron.

maple*
[méipl]

n. 단풍나무
A maple or a maple tree is a tree with five-pointed leaves which turn bright red or gold in autumn.

surround**
[səráund]

v. 둘러싸다, 에워싸다; 포위하다
If a person or thing is surrounded by something, that thing is situated all around them.

worn**
[wɔ:rn]

a. 닳아 해진, 써서 낡은; 지쳐버린, 수척해진
Worn is used to describe something that is damaged or thin because it is old and has been used a lot.

courteous*
[kə́:rtiəs]

a. 정중한, 공손한
Someone who is courteous is polite and respectful to other people.

manner*
[mǽnər]

n. (사람의) 태도; (일의) 방식; (사회 · 문화의) 예의
Someone's manner is the way in which they behave and talk when they are with other people, for example whether they are polite, confident, or bad-tempered.

principal*
[prínsəpəl]

n. 교장; **a.** 주요한, 주된
The principal of a school or college is the person in charge of the school or college.

nudge
[nʌdʒ]

n. 쿡 찌르기; **v.** (살짝) 쿡 찌르다; 조금씩 밀다; 밀치고 나아가다
A nudge is a gentle push, usually with an elbow, in order to draw someone's attention to something.

closet*
[klázit]

n. 벽장
A closet is a piece of furniture with doors at the front and shelves inside, which is used for storing things.

exclaim*
[ikskléim]

v. 소리치다, 외치다
If you exclaim, you cry out suddenly in surprise, strong emotion, or pain.

incredulous
[inkrédʒuləs]

a. 믿지 않는, 못 믿겠다는 듯한 (incredulously **ad.** 믿을 수 없다는 듯이)
If someone is incredulous, they are unable to believe something because it is very surprising or shocking.

bet*
[bet]

v. (~이) 틀림없다; (경마 · 내기 등에) 돈을 걸다; **n.** 내기; 내기 돈
You use an expression 'I bet' to indicate that you are sure something is true.

stolid
[stálid]

a. 둔감한, 무신경한 (stolidly **ad.** 둔감하게, 무신경하게)
If you describe someone as stolid, you mean that they do not show much emotion or are not very exciting or interesting.

burst into

idiom (갑자기) ~을 터뜨리다
If you burst into something, you start producing or doing it suddenly and with great force.

shriek*
[ʃriːk]

n. (날카롭게 지르는) 비명; **v.** (날카롭게) 비명을 지르다; 악을 쓰며 말하다
A shriek is a short, very loud cry.

peal
[piːl]

n. (울리듯 이어지는) 큰 소리; **v.** 우렁차게 울리다
A peal of laughter or thunder consists of a long, loud series of sounds.

laughter^{복습}
[lǽftər]

n. 웃음, 웃기; 웃음소리
Laughter is the sound of people laughing, for example because they are amused or happy.

obvious**
[ábviəs]

a. 분명한, 명백한; 확실한; 너무 빤한 (obviously **ad.** 확실히, 분명히)
You use obviously when you are stating something that you expect the person who is listening to know already.

derisive
[diráisiv]

a. 조소하는, 조롱하는 (derisively **ad.** 비웃듯이, 조소하며)
A derisive noise, expression, or remark expresses contempt.

ivy
[áivi]

n. 담쟁이덩굴
Ivy is an evergreen plant that grows up walls or along the ground.

brick**
[brik]

n. 벽돌
Bricks are rectangular blocks of baked clay used for building walls, which are usually red or brown.

exaggerated
[igzǽdʒərèitid]

a. (행동이) 과장된; 과장된, 부풀린, 지나친
Something that is exaggerated is or seems larger, better, worse, or more important than it actually needs to be.

polite***
[pəláit]

a. 예의 바른, 공손한, 정중한 (politeness n. 공손함)
Someone who is polite has good manners and behaves in a way that is socially correct and not rude to other people.

greet**
[gri:t]

v. 반응을 보이다; 환영하다
If something is greeted in a particular way, people react to it in that way.

shift*
[ʃift]

v. 자세를 바꾸다; (장소를) 옮기다; (견해 · 방식을) 바꾸다; n. 변화
If you shift something or if it shifts, it moves slightly.

distant**
[dístənt]

a. 먼, (멀리) 떨어져 있는; 다정하지 않은
Distant means very far away.

spot**
[spat]

n. (특정한) 곳; (작은) 점; v. 발견하다, 찾다, 알아채다
You can refer to a particular place as a spot.

outer**
[áutər]

a. (안 · 중심에서 가장) 바깥쪽의, 외곽의; 바깥 표면의
The outer parts of something are the parts which contain or enclose the other parts, and which are furthest from the center.

fringe*
[frindʒ]

n. (지역 · 그룹의) 주변부, 변두리; v. 가장자리를 형성하다
To be on the fringe or the fringes of a place means to be on the outside edge of it, or to be in one of the parts that are farthest from its center.

break away

idiom (~에서) 떨어지다; (~에서) 달아나다
To break away means to move away from a group of people or a crowd.

gradual*
[grǽdʒuəl]

a. 점진적인, 서서히 일어나는; 완만한 (gradually ad. 서서히)
If something changes or is done gradually, it changes or is done in small stages over a long period of time, rather than suddenly.

disperse
[dispɔ́:rs]

v. (이리저리) 흩어지다, 해산하다; 해산시키다; (넓은 지역에) 흩어지다
When a group of people disperses or when someone disperses them, the group splits up and the people leave in different directions.

inseparable
[insépərəbl]

a. (사람 사이를) 갈라놓을 수 없는; 불가분한
If you say that two people are inseparable, you are emphasizing that they are very good friends and spend a great deal of time together.

dull**
[dʌl]

a. 흐릿한; 따분한, 재미없는; 무딘; 둔한
Someone or something that is dull is not very lively or energetic.

hitch
[hiʧ]

v. (위로) 몸을 올리다; (지나가는 차를) 얻어 타다
If you hitch a part of your body or something that you are carrying, you move it to a higher position.

every now and then

idiom 때때로, 가끔
If you say that something happens every now and then, you mean that it happens sometimes but not very often or regularly.

cruel**
[kru:əl]

a. 잔혹한, 잔인한; 고통스러운, 괴로운
Someone who is cruel deliberately causes pain or distress to people or animals.

bully*
[búli]

n. (약자를) 괴롭히는 사람; v. (약자를) 괴롭히다; 협박하다
A bully is someone who uses their strength or power to hurt or frighten other people.

mistreat
[mistrí:t]

v. (사람 · 동물을) 학대하다, 혹사하다
If someone mistreats a person or an animal, they treat them badly, especially by making them suffer physically.

ordinary**
[ɔ́:rdənèri]

a. 평범한; 보통의, 일상적인
Ordinary people or things are normal and not special or different in any way.

bother*
[báðər]

v. 신경 쓰이게 하다, 괴롭히다; 애를 쓰다; 귀찮게 하다, 귀찮게 말을 걸다; n. 성가심
If something bothers you, or if you bother about it, it worries, annoys, or upsets you.

hand-me-down
[hǽnd-mi-dàun]

a. 헌 옷의
Hand-me-down is used to describe things, especially clothes, which have been used by someone else before you and which have been given to you for your use.

goodness*
[gúdnis]

int. 와!, 어머나!, 맙소사!; n. 신; 선량함 (thank goodness int. 정말 다행이다)
'Thank goodness' is used as an expression of relief.

forehead*
[fɔ́:rhèd]

n. 이마
Your forehead is the area at the front of your head between your eyebrows and your hair.

mock*
[mak]

a. 거짓된, 가짜의; v. 놀리다, 조롱하다; 무시하다
You use mock to describe something which is not real or genuine, but which is intended to be very similar to the real thing.

embarrass**
[imbǽrəs]

v. 당황스럽게 하다; 곤란하게 하다 (embarrassed a. 어색한, 당황스러운)
A person who is embarrassed feels shy, ashamed, or guilty about something.

marble*
[ma:rbl]

n. (아이들이 가지고 노는) 구슬; 대리석
A marble is a small ball, usually made of colored or transparent glass, that is used in children's games.

palm*
[pa:m]

n. 손바닥; 야자과 나무, 종려나무
The palm of your hand is the inside part.

exact**
[igzǽkt]

a. 정확한, 정밀한 (exactly ad. 정확히, 꼭, 틀림없이)
You can use not exactly to show that you mean the opposite of what you are saying.

24

attention[**]
[əténʃən]

n. 관심, 흥미; 주의, 주목; v. 알립니다, 주목하세요
(pay attention idiom 관심을 갖다)
If you pay attention to someone, you watch them, listen to them, or take notice of them.

invent[**]
[invént]

v. 발명하다; (사실이 아닌 것을) 지어내다
If you invent something such as a machine or process, you are the first person to think of it or make it.

sense[***]
[sens]

n. 지각, 일리; 감각; v. 감지하다, 느끼다
(have more sense than to idiom ~하지 않을 정도로 분별이 있다)
Sense is the ability to make good judgments and to behave sensibly.

tease[*]
[tiːz]

v. 놀리다, 장난하다; (동물을) 못 살게 굴다; n. 장난, 놀림
To tease someone means to laugh at them or make jokes about them in order to embarrass, annoy, or upset them.

chapter three

1. Why was it hard for Maddie to focus on her work in class?
   A. She had forgotten to bring a pencil to class.
   B. She had forgotten to bring her notebook.
   C. She had been late and lost her homework.
   D. She had been late and was thinking of Wanda.

2. How was the weather on the day the dresses game started?
   A. It was a bright blue day in September.
   B. It was a bright blue day in October.
   C. It was a cloudy gray day in September.
   D. It was a cloudy gray day in October.

3. Why were the girls gathered around Cecile?
   A. Cecile was showing off her dancing skills.
   B. Cecile was telling an interesting story.
   C. Cecile was wearing a bright new dress.
   D. Cecile was inviting the girls to her birthday party.

4. Why did Cecile wear fancier clothes than most of them?
   A. She was very rich.
   B. She was a toe dancer.
   C. She worked at a clothing store.
   D. She made her own dresses.

5. Why did Jake and Wanda rarely come to school together?

   A. They went to different schools on opposite sides of town.

   B. Wanda wanted to walk to school with her friends.

   C. Wanda had to get to school early to help Miss Mason.

   D. Jake had to get to school early to help the school janitor.

6. Why did Maddie think that Wanda told Peggy about her dresses?

   A. Maddie thought that maybe Wanda would really be one of the girls.

   B. Maddie thought that maybe Wanda was jealous of Cecile's dress.

   C. Maddie thought that maybe Wanda wanted Peggy to laugh at her.

   D. Maddie thought that maybe Wanda wanted to impress Peggy.

7. How did Peggy feel about asking Wanda about her dresses after the first time?

   A. Peggy got bored and completely forgot about it the next day.

   B. Peggy felt like a day was lost if she had not asked Wanda about it.

   C. Peggy felt bad about laughing at Wanda and apologized the next day.

   D. Peggy felt like asking Wanda every day until she showed them her dresses.

1분에 몇 단어를 읽는지 리딩 속도를 측정해보세요.

$$\frac{1{,}474 \text{ words}}{\text{reading time (\quad) sec}} \times 60 = (\quad) \text{ WPM}$$

Build Your Vocabulary

somehow**
[sʌ́mhàu]
ad. 왜 그런지 (모르겠지만), 왠지; 어떻게든
You use somehow to say that you do not know or cannot say how something was done or will be done.

buckle*
[bʌkl]
v. 버클로 잠그다; 찌그러지다, 휘어지다; n. 버클, 잠금 장치
(buckle down **idiom** 본격적으로 덤비다, 착수하다)
To buckle down to something means to start working or doing something in a serious or determined way.

sharpen*
[ʃáːrpən]
v. (날카롭게) 갈다, 깎다; 선명해지다, 날카로워지다 (sharpener n. ～을 깎는 기구)
If you sharpen an object, you make its edge very thin or you make its end pointed.

shaving
[ʃéiviŋ]
n. (pl.) 깎아낸 부스러기, 대팻밥
Shavings are small very thin pieces of wood or other material which have been cut from a larger piece.

neat**
[niːt]
a. 정돈된, 단정한; 깔끔한; 뛰어난
A neat place, thing, or person is tidy and smart, and has everything in the correct place.

heap*
[hiːp]
n. 더미, 무더기; 많음; v. (아무렇게나) 쌓다; 쌓아 올리다
A heap of things is a pile of them, especially a pile arranged in a rather untidy way.

scrap*
[skræp]
n. (종이 · 옷감 등의) 조각; 폐품; v. 폐기하다, 버리다
A scrap of something is a very small piece or amount of it.

dust***
[dʌst]
n. (흙)먼지; v. 먼지를 털다
Dust is a fine powder which consists of very small particles of a substance such as gold, wood, or coal.

lead**
[led]
n. (연필)심; 납
The lead in a pencil is the center part of it which makes a mark on paper.

arithmetic*
[əríθmətik]
n. 산수, 연산; 산술, 계산
Arithmetic is the part of mathematics that is concerned with the addition, subtraction, multiplication, and division of numbers.

slight**
[slait]
a. 약간의, 조금의; 작고 여윈, 가냘픈
Something that is slight is very small in degree or quantity.

frown*
[fraun]

n. 찡그림, 찌푸림; **v.** 얼굴을 찡그리다; 눈살을 찌푸리다
A frown is a facial expression made by drawing your eyebrows together that shows you are annoyed or worried.

pucker
[pʌkər]

v. 주름을 잡다, 구겨지다; (입술 등을) 오므리다; **n.** 주름
When a part of your face puckers or when you pucker it, it becomes tight or stretched, often because you are trying not to cry or are going to kiss someone.

forehead^{복습}
[fɔ́ːrhèd]

n. 이마
Your forehead is the area at the front of your head between your eyebrows and your hair.

in the first place

idiom 우선, 먼저; 애초에
You say in the first place and in the second place to introduce the first and second in a series of points or reasons.

impatient*
[impéiʃənt]

a. 어서 ~하고 싶어 하는; 짜증난, 안달하는 (impatiently **ad.** 성급하게, 조바심하며)
If you are impatient, you are annoyed because you have to wait too long for something.

scene**
[siːn]

n. 장면, 광경; 현장; 풍경
You refer to a place as a scene when you are describing its appearance and indicating what impression it makes on you.

flash**
[flæʃ]

v. (감정·생각 등이) 갑자기 떠오르다; (잠깐) 비치다, 번쩍이다; 휙 움직이다; **n.** 섬광, 번쩍임; 순간
If something flashes through or into your mind, you suddenly think about it.

swift*
[swift]

a. 신속한, 재빠른; 빠른, 날랜 (swiftly **ad.** 신속히, 빨리)
Something that is swift moves very quickly.

vivid*
[vívid]

a. 생생한; 선명한, 강렬한 (vividly **ad.** 생생하게, 선명하게)
If you describe memories and descriptions as vivid, you mean that they are very clear and detailed.

afterwards*
[ǽftərwərdz]

ad. 나중에, 그 뒤에
If you do something or if something happens afterwards, you do it or it happens after a particular event or time that has already been mentioned.

shady*
[ʃéidi]

a. (빛이 바로 닿지 않게) 그늘이 드리워진
You can describe a place as shady when you like the fact that it is sheltered from bright sunlight, for example by trees or buildings.

blink*
[bliŋk]

v. 눈을 깜박이다; (불빛이) 깜박거리다; **n.** 눈을 깜박거림
When you blink or when you blink your eyes, you shut your eyes and very quickly open them again.

besides**
[bisáidz]

prep. ~외에; **ad.** 게다가, 뿐만 아니라
Besides something or beside something means in addition to it.

dozen**
[dʌzn]

n. 십여 명, 십여 개; 12개짜리 한 묶음, 다스; (pl.) 다수, 여러 개
You can refer to a group of approximately six things or people as half a dozen.

crimson
[krímzn]

a. 진홍색
Something that is crimson is deep red in color.

particular**
[pərtíkjulər]

a. 특정한; (보통보다 더 많거나 대단하여) 특별한
You use particular to emphasize that you are talking about one thing or one kind of thing rather than other similar ones.

ray*
[rei]

n. 광선; 약간, 소량
Rays of light are narrow beams of light.

crisp*
[krisp]

a. 상쾌한; (식품이) 바삭바삭한; n. 감자칩
Weather that is pleasantly fresh, cold, and dry can be described as crisp.

swish
[swiʃ]

v. 휙 소리를 내며 움직이다; 휘두르다; n. 휙 하는 소리
If something swishes or if you swish it, it moves quickly through the air, making a soft sound.

exclaim^{복습}
[ikskléim]

v. 소리치다, 외치다
If you exclaim, you cry out suddenly in surprise, strong emotion, or pain.

greet^{복습}
[gri:t]

v. 환영하다; 반응을 보이다
When you greet someone, you say 'Hello' or shake hands with them.

admire**
[ædmáiər]

v. 칭찬하다, 존경하다; 감탄하며 바라보다
If you admire someone or something, you look at them with pleasure.

slender*
[sléndər]

a. 호리호리한, 가느다란, 날씬한
A slender person is attractively thin and graceful.

toe*
[tou]

n. 발가락
Your toes are the five movable parts at the end of each foot.

fancy**
[fǽnsi]

a. 장식이 많은, 색깔이 화려한; 고급의; v. 생각하다, 상상하다
If you describe something as fancy, you mean that it is special, unusual, or elaborate, for example because it has a lot of decoration.

precious*
[préʃəs]

a. 소중한; 귀중한, 값비싼; ad. 정말 거의 없는
If something is precious to you, you regard it as important and do not want to lose it.

sling
[sliŋ]

v. (slung–slung) (느슨하게) 매다, 걸다; 던지다; n. 팔걸이 붕대
If you sling something over your shoulder or over something such as a chair, you hang it there loosely.

shoelace
[ʃúːleis]

n. 구두끈, 신발끈
Shoelaces are long, narrow pieces of material like pieces of string that you use to fasten your shoes.

jolly*
[dʒáli]

a. 행복한, 쾌활한; 즐거운
Someone who is jolly is happy and cheerful in their appearance or behavior.

sparkle*
[spa:rkl]

v. 반짝이다; 생기 넘치다; n. 반짝거림, 광채
If something sparkles, it is clear and bright and shines with a lot of very small points of light.

shimmer
[ʃímər]
v. 희미하게 빛나다; n. 희미한 빛
If something shimmers, it shines with a faint, unsteady light or has an unclear, unsteady appearance.

bay*
[bei]
n. 만(灣); 구역, 구간; 월계수 잎
A bay is a part of a coast where the land curves inward.

edge**
[edʒ]
v. 테두리를 두르다; 조금씩 움직이다; n. 끝, 가장자리; 우위
If something is edged with a particular thing, that thing forms a border around it.

pole**
[poul]
n. 막대기, 기둥, 장대; 극
A pole is a long thin piece of wood or metal, used especially for supporting things.

janitor
[dʒǽnitər]
n. (건물의) 관리인, 잡역부
A janitor is a person whose job is to look after a building.

furnace*
[fɔ́:rnis]
n. 보일러
A furnace is a device which burns gas, oil, electricity, or coal in order to provide hot water, especially for the central heating in a building.

rake*
[reik]
v. 갈퀴질을 하다, 갈퀴로 모으다; n. 갈퀴
If you rake leaves or ashes, you move them somewhere using a rake or a similar tool.

odd**
[ad]
a. 이상한, 특이한; 홀수의
If you describe someone or something as odd, you think that they are strange or unusual.

pale**
[peil]
a. (색깔이) 옅은; 창백한, 핼쑥한; v. 창백해지다
If something is pale, it is very light in color or almost white.

jaunty
[dʒɔ́:nti]
a. 쾌활한, 의기양양한, 경쾌한
If you describe someone or something as jaunty, you mean that they are full of confidence and energy.

absentminded*
[æbsəntmáindid]
a. 멍하니 있는, 넋놓은, 방심 상태의 (absentmindedly ad. 멍하니, 넋을 잃고)
Someone who is absentminded forgets things or does not pay attention to what they are doing.

stop short
idiom (하던 일을) 갑자기 멈추다
To stop short means to suddenly stop doing something.

shrug*
[ʃrʌg]
v. (어깨를) 으쓱하다; n. 어깨를 으쓱하기
If you shrug, you raise your shoulders to show that you are not interested in something or that you do not know or care about something.

forward**
[fɔ́:rwərd]
ad. 앞으로; 더 일찍;
v. (이사 간 사람에게 배달된 편지 등을 새 주소로) 다시 보내 주다; 전달하다
If you move or look forward, you move or look in a direction that is in front of you.

hesitate***
[hézətèit]

v. 망설이다, 주저하다
If you hesitate, you do not speak or act for a short time, usually because you are uncertain, embarrassed, or worried about what you are going to say or do.

timid*
[tímid]

a. 소심한, 자신감이 없는
Timid people are shy, nervous, and have no courage or confidence in themselves.

alarm*
[əláːrm]

v. 불안하게 하다; n. 불안, 공포; 경보(음), 경고 신호
If something alarms you, it makes you afraid or anxious that something unpleasant or dangerous might happen.

twist복습
[twist]

v. 비틀다, 일그러뜨리다; (고개 · 몸 등을) 돌리다; 구부리다;
n. (고개 · 몸 등을) 돌리기
If you twist something, especially a part of your body, it moves into an unusual, uncomfortable, or bent position, for example because of being hit or pushed, or because you are upset.

vague*
[veig]

a. 희미한, 어렴풋한; 모호한, 애매한
A vague shape or outline is not clear and is therefore not easy to see.

suggest***
[səgdʒést]

v. 말하다, (뜻을) 비치다; (아이디어 · 계획을) 제안하다; 추천하다
(suggestion n. 기미, 기색)
If there is a suggestion of something, there is a slight amount or sign of it.

fringe복습
[frindʒ]

n. (지역 · 그룹의) 주변부, 변두리; v. 가장자리를 형성하다
To be on the fringe or the fringes of a place means to be on the outside edge of it, or to be in one of the parts that are farthest from its center.

enlarge**
[inláːrdʒ]

v. 확대하다, 확장하다
When you enlarge something or when it enlarges, it becomes bigger.

plaid
[plæd]

n. 격자 무늬 천; 격자 무늬
Plaid is material with a check design on it. Plaid is also the design itself.

at once

idiom 동시에; 즉시
If a number of different things happen at once or all at once, they all happen at the same time.

envelop
[invéləp]

v. 감싸다, 뒤덮다
If one thing envelops another, it covers or surrounds it completely.

figure***
[fígjər]

v. (~일 거라고) 생각하다; (어떤 과정 · 상황 등에서) 중요하다; n. 수치; 숫자
If you figure that something is the case, you think or guess that it is the case.

all of a sudden

idiom 갑자기
If something happens all of a sudden, it happens quickly and unexpectedly.

impulsive
[impÁlsiv]

a. 충동적인 (impulsively ad. 충동적으로)
If you describe someone as impulsive, you mean that they do things suddenly without thinking about them carefully first.

32

firm***
[fə:rm]

a. 단호한, 단단한; 딱딱한; 확고한; **n.** 회사 (firmly **ad.** 단호히)
If you describe someone as firm, you mean they behave in a way that shows that they are not going to change their mind, or that they are the person who is in control.

yell*
[jel]

v. 소리치다, 소리 지르다, 외치다; **n.** 고함, 외침
If you yell, you shout loudly, usually because you are excited, angry, or in pain.

finery
[fáinəri]

n. (특히 특별한 경우에 입는) 화려한 옷, 아름다운 장식품
If someone is dressed in their finery, they are wearing the elegant and impressive clothes and jewelry that they wear on special occasions.

curious**
[kjúəriəs]

a. 궁금한, 호기심이 많은; 별난, 특이한 (curiously **ad.** 신기한 듯이)
If you are curious about something, you are interested in it and want to know more about it.

incredulous^{복습}
[inkrédʒuləs]

a. 믿지 않는, 못 믿겠다는 듯한 (incredulously **ad.** 믿을 수 없다는 듯이)
If someone is incredulous, they are unable to believe something because it is very surprising or shocking.

suspicious*
[səspíʃəs]

a. 의혹을 갖는, 수상쩍어 하는; 의심스러운
(suspiciously **ad.** 수상쩍게; 미심쩍다는 듯이)
If you are suspicious of someone or something, you do not trust them, and are careful when dealing with them.

closet^{복습}
[klázit]

n. 벽장
A closet is a piece of furniture with doors at the front and shelves inside, which is used for storing things.

stolid^{복습}
[stálid]

a. 둔감한, 무신경한 (stolidly **ad.** 둔감하게, 무신경하게)
If you describe someone as stolid, you mean that they do not show much emotion or are not very exciting or interesting.

grown-up*
[gróun-ʌp]

a. (사람이) 다 큰, 장성한, 어른이 된
If you say that someone is grown-up, you mean that they behave in an adult way, often when they are in fact still a child.

chalk**
[tʃɔ:k]

n. 분필
Chalk is small sticks of soft white rock, used for writing or drawing with.

purse*
[pə:rs]

v. (입술을) 오므리다; **n.** 지갑; 돈, 자금
If you purse your lips, you move them into a small, rounded shape, usually because you disapprove of something or when you are thinking.

wrinkle*
[riŋkl]

v. (얼굴에) 주름을 잡다, 찡그리다; **n.** 주름, 잔주름
When you wrinkle your nose or forehead, or when it wrinkles, you tighten the muscles in your face so that the skin folds.

slip^{복습}
[slip]

v. 미끄러지다; 빠져 나가다; (들키지 않고) 슬며시 가다; **n.** (작은) 실수; 미끄러짐
If something slips, it slides out of place or out of your hand.

gong
[gɔ:ŋ]

n. (악기 · 신호용) 징
A gong is a large, flat, circular piece of metal that you hit with a hammer to make a sound like a loud bell.

warn***
[wɔːrn]

v. 경고하다, 주의를 주다 (warning n. 경고)
A warning is something which is said or written to tell people of a possible danger, problem, or other unpleasant thing that might happen.

relieve*
[rilíːv]

v. 안도하게 하다; (불쾌감·고통 등을) 없애 주다; 완화하다 (relieved a. 안도하는)
If you are relieved, you feel happy because something unpleasant has not happened or is no longer happening.

laughter^{복습}
[lǽftər]

n. 웃음, 웃기; 웃음소리
Laughter is the sound of people laughing, for example because they are amused or happy.

approve*
[əprúːv]

v. 찬성하다, 괜찮다고 생각하다 (approving a. 찬성하는, 좋다고 여기는)
An approving reaction or remark shows support for something, or satisfaction with it.

unexpected**
[ʌnikspéktid]

a. 예기치 않은, 예상 밖의 (unexpectedly ad. 갑자기, 뜻밖에)
If an event or someone's behavior is unexpected, it surprises you because you did not think that it was likely to happen.

wag*
[wæg]

v. (흔히 불만스럽다는 뜻으로 손가락·고개를) 흔들다; (개가 꼬리를) 흔들다;
n. 흔들기
If you wag your head, you move it from side to side, often because you are unhappy about a situation.

wrap**
[ræp]

v. (포장지 등으로) 싸다, 포장하다; n. 포장지
When you wrap something, you fold paper or cloth tightly round it to cover it completely, for example in order to protect it or so that you can give it to someone as a present.

chapter four

1. Why was Maddie glad even though she had been late to school?
   A. She was glad that she missed the morning session.
   B. She was glad that she had not had to make fun of Wanda.
   C. She was glad that she had not had to stay after school.
   D. She was glad that it was a bright and sunny day.

2. Why did Maddie want to write Peggy a note?
   A. She wanted to practice her note writing to friends.
   B. She wanted Peggy to help to write an apology to Wanda.
   C. She didn't have courage to speak out right to Peggy.
   D. She thought that Peggy would take her ideas more seriously.

3. Why did Maddie decide against writing a note?
   A. She worried that Peggy would make her a new target.
   B. She wanted to pay attention to her teacher's lesson.
   C. She wanted to talk to Peggy directly about Wanda.
   D. She wanted to keep asking Wanda about her dresses.

4. How did Maddie ultimately feel about Peggy making fun of Wanda?
   A. She felt that Miss Mason would tell Peggy to stop bullying Wanda.
   B. She felt that Peggy would get bored of asking Wanda about her dresses.

C. She felt that the other girls would tell Peggy to stop making fun of Wanda.

D. She felt that Peggy would have to decide for herself to stop making fun of Wanda.

5. How did the other students feel about Wanda reading in class?

A. They hoped that she would hurry up and finish, because she read slowly.

B. They hoped that she would slow down, because she read too quickly.

C. They hoped that she would read more, because they liked her voice.

D. They hoped that she would not study at all before standing and speaking.

6. When was the only time Wanda really talked?

A. She only really talked to Maddie after school about friends.

B. She only really talked in the school yard about her dresses.

C. She only really talked in class about reading assignments.

D. She only really talked between classes with her brother Jake.

7. How did Maddie feel about the drawing and color contest?

A. She felt that Peggy would probably win the girls' medal.

B. She felt that she had a good chance of winning this year.

C. She felt that boys and girls should both draw motorboats.

D. She felt that Wanda might win because she knew about dresses.

1분에 몇 단어를 읽는지 리딩 속도를 측정해보세요.

$$\frac{548 \text{ words}}{\text{reading time ( ) sec}} \times 60 = (\quad) \text{ WPM}$$

Build Your Vocabulary

make fun of

idiom ~을 놀리다
If you make fun of someone or something you laugh at them, tease them, or make jokes about them in a way that causes them to seem ridiculous.

arithmetic^{복습}
[əríθmətik]

n. 산수, 연산; 산술, 계산
Arithmetic is the part of mathematics that is concerned with the addition, subtraction, multiplication, and division of numbers.

absentminded^{복습}
[æbsəntmáindid]

a. 멍하니 있는, 넋놓은, 방심 상태의 (absentmindedly ad. 멍하니, 넋을 잃고)
Someone who is absentminded forgets things or does not pay attention to what they are doing.

nerve^{**}
[nə:rv]

n. (어려움에 맞서는) 대담성, 용기; 신경
Nerve is the courage that you need in order to do something difficult or dangerous.

courage^{***}
[kə́:ridʒ]

n. 용기
Courage is the quality shown by someone who decides to do something difficult or dangerous, even though they may be afraid.

speak out

idiom (~에 반대하는 뜻을) 공개적으로 말하다
If you speak out, you say what you think clearly and publicly, often criticizing or opposing someone or something.

pause^{**}
[pɔ:z]

v. (말·일을 하다가) 잠시 멈추다; 정지시키다; n. (말·행동 등의) 멈춤
If you pause while you are doing something, you stop for a short period and then continue.

shudder[*]
[ʃʌdər]

v. (공포·추위 등으로) 몸을 떨다; 마구 흔들리다;
n. 몸이 떨림, 전율; 크게 흔들림
If you shudder, you shake with fear, horror, or disgust, or because you are cold.

picture^{***}
[píktʃər]

v. ~을 상상하다, 마음속에 그리다; n. 그림; 사진
If you picture something in your mind, you think of it and have such a clear memory or idea of it that you seem to be able to see it.

yard^{복습}
[ja:rd]

n. (학교의) 운동장; 마당, 뜰; 정원 (school yard n. 학교 운동장)
The school yard is the large open area with a hard surface just outside a school building, where the schoolchildren can play and do other activities.

38

disguise*
[disgáiz]

v. 위장하다, 숨기다; 변장하다; n. 변장, 위장
To disguise something means to hide it or make it appear different so that people will not know about it or will not recognize it.

trim*
[trim]

v. (특히 가장자리를) 장식하다; 다듬다, 정돈하다, 손질하다
(trimming n. (테두리 등의) 장식)
The trimming on something such as a piece of clothing is the decoration, for example along its edges, that is in a different color or material.

recognize**
[rékəgnàiz]

v. 알아보다; 인식하다; 공인하다
If you recognize someone or something, you know who that person is or what that thing is.

of one's own accord

idiom 자발적으로, 자진해서; 저절로, 자연히
If you do something of your own accord, you do it because you want to, without being asked or forced.

blond*
[bland]

a. (머리가) 금발인
Blond hair can be very light brown or light yellow.

tear**
[tɛər]

① v. (tore-torn) 찢다, 뜯다; 뜯어 내다; n. 찢어진 곳, 구멍 ② n. 눈물
If you tear something to pieces, you completely destroy it.

bit**
[bit]

n. 작은 조각, 조각; 조금, 약간
A bit of something is a small piece of it.

except복습
[iksépt]

prep. (누구·무엇을) 제외하고는
You use except to introduce the only thing or person that a statement does not apply to, or a fact that prevents a statement from being completely true.

oral*
[ɔ́:rəl]

a. 구두의; 구술의; n. 구두시험
Oral communication is spoken rather than written.

paragraph*
[pǽrəgræf]

n. 단락, 절
A paragraph is a section of a piece of writing. A paragraph always begins on a new line and contains at least one sentence.

dumb*
[dʌm]

a. 멍청한, 바보 같은; 말을 못 하는
If you say that something is dumb, you think that it is silly and annoying.

timid복습
[tímid]

a. 소심한, 자신감이 없는
Timid people are shy, nervous, and have no courage or confidence in themselves.

pale복습
[peil]

a. (색깔이) 옅은; 창백한, 핼쑥한; v. 창백해지다
If something is pale, it is very light in color or almost white.

brilliant*
[bríljənt]

a. (빛·색깔이) 아주 밝은; 훌륭한, 멋진
A brilliant color is extremely bright.

pretend***
[priténd]

v. ~인 척하다, ~인 것처럼 굴다; ~라고 가장하다 (pretended a. 거짓의)
If something is pretended, it is not genuine or sincere.

admire^{복습}
[ædmáiər]

v. 감탄하며 바라보다; 칭찬하다, 존경하다 (admiration n. 감탄, 존경)
Admiration is a feeling of great liking and respect for a person or thing.

contest[*]
[kántest]

n. 대회, 시합
A contest is a competition or game in which people try to win.

consist^{**}
[kənsíst]

v. (부분 · 요소로) 이루어져 있다
Something that consists of particular things or people is formed from them.

announce^{**}
[ənáuns]

v. 발표하다, 알리다; (공공장소에서) 방송하다
If you announce something, you tell people about it publicly or officially.

sink^{***}
[siŋk]

v. (양 · 강도 등이) 약해지다; 가라앉다, 빠지다; n. (부엌의) 싱크대, 개수대
If something sinks to a lower level or standard, it falls to that level or standard.

chapter five

1. Why did Peggy and Maddie want to get to school on time?
   A. They wanted to stay dry before it started raining.
   B. They wanted to see who would win the drawing contest.
   C. They wanted to make up for being late the previous day.
   D. They wanted to see if Wanda would come to school.

2. Why were Peggy and Maddie surprised when they entered the classroom?
   A. Wanda had returned to school.
   B. Maddie had won the drawing and color contest.
   C. A hundred drawings of dresses were hung around the room.
   D. All of the other students had already arrived and had begun class.

3. How did the judges feel about Wanda's drawings?
   A. They felt that she should have only submitted one or two.
   B. They felt that any one of her drawings would have won.
   C. They felt that she must have owned a hundred real dresses.
   D. They felt that she could be a famous fashion designer.

4. How did the children react to Wanda winning?
   A. They were sad that Wanda was absent.
   B. They burst into laughter and mocked her drawings.
   C. They burst into applause and admired her drawings.
   D. They hoped that Wanda would share her drawings.

5. Why had Wanda's father written a note to her teacher?
   A. He let the teacher know that they all moved away to the big city.
   B. He let the teacher know that Wanda and Jake were sick at home.
   C. He let the teacher know that Maddie and Peggy had bullied Wanda.
   D. He let the teacher know that everyone had been nice to them about their name.

6. How did Maddie feel after Miss Mason had read the note?
   A. She felt that she and Peggy had done nothing wrong.
   B. She felt that she had been a coward in just standing by.
   C. She felt that Miss Mason was specifically targeting her as a bully.
   D. She felt that she had done nothing wrong because she had only made fun of Wanda's dresses.

7. Why did Maddie feel that Peggy was really all right when school was over for the day?
   A. Peggy had the same idea of writing a note to Wanda.
   B. Peggy had the same idea of bringing Wanda her medal.
   C. Peggy had the same idea of drawing a dress for Wanda.
   D. Peggy had the same idea of visiting Wanda's house.

$$\frac{1,017 \text{ words}}{\text{reading time ( ) sec}} \times 60 = (\quad) \text{ WPM}$$

Build Your Vocabulary

drizzle
[drizl]

v. (비가) 보슬보슬 내리다; (액체를) 조금 붓다; n. 이슬비, 가랑비
If it is drizzling, it is raining very lightly.

naturally*
[nǽtʃərəli]

ad. 물론, 당연히, 자연스럽게; 자연 발생적으로, 저절로
You use naturally to indicate that you think something is very obvious and not at all surprising in the circumstances.

railroad**
[réilroud]

n. 철로, 철길
A railroad is a route between two places along which trains travel on steel rails.

track복습
[træk]

n. (기차) 선로; 길; 자국; v. 발자국을 남기다; 추적하다; (자취 등을 따라) 뒤쫓다
Railway tracks are the rails that a train travels along.

height복습
[hait]

n. 높은 곳; (사물의) 높이; (사람의) 키
A height is a high position or place above the ground.

take a chance

idiom (~을) 운에 맡기다
When you take a chance, you try to do something although there is a large risk of danger or failure.

announce복습
[ənáuns]

v. 발표하다, 알리다; (공공장소에서) 방송하다
If you announce something, you tell people about it publicly or officially.

eager***
[íːgər]

a. 열렬한, 간절히 바라는, 열심인 (eagerly ad. 열망하여)
If you are eager to do or have something, you want to do or have it very much.

gasp*
[gæsp]

v. 숨이 턱 막히다, 헉 하고 숨을 쉬다; 숨을 제대로 못 쉬다; n. 헉 하는 소리를 냄
When you gasp, you take a short quick breath through your mouth, especially when you are surprised, shocked, or in pain.

ledge*
[ledʒ]

n. (벽에서 튀어나온) 선반; 절벽에서 튀어나온 바위
A ledge is a narrow shelf along the bottom edge of a window.

windowsill
[wíndousil]

n. 창턱
A windowsill is a shelf along the bottom of a window, either inside or outside a building.

tack
[tæk]

v. 압정으로 고정시키다; n. 압정
If you tack something to a surface, you pin it there with tacks or drawing pins.

blackboard
[blǽkbɔ̀:rd]

n. 칠판
A blackboard is a dark-colored board that you can write on with chalk.

spread***
[spred]

v. 펼치다, 펴다; 퍼지다, 확산되다
If you spread something somewhere, you open it out or arrange it over a place or surface, so that all of it can be seen or used easily.

dazzle*
[dǽzl]

v. 눈부시게 하다; n. 눈부심 (dazzling a. 눈부신)
Something that is dazzling is very impressive or beautiful.

brilliant^{복습}
[bríljənt]

a. 훌륭한, 멋진; 빛나는, 찬란한
A brilliant person, idea, or performance is extremely clever or skillful.

lavish
[lǽviʃ]

a. 호화로운; 풍성한; 아주 후한
If you describe something as lavish, you mean that it is very elaborate and impressive and a lot of money has been spent on it.

sheet**
[ʃi:t]

n. (종이) 한 장; 시트(침대에 깔거나 위로 덮는 얇은 천)
A sheet of paper is a rectangular piece of paper.

wrap^{복습}
[ræp]

v. (포장지 등으로) 싸다, 포장하다; n. 포장지 (wrapping paper n. 포장지)
Wrapping paper is special paper which is used for wrapping presents.

contest^{복습}
[kántest]

n. 대회, 시합
A contest is a competition or game in which people try to win.

whistle**
[hwisl]

v. 휘파람을 불다; 기적을 울리다; n. (기차·배 등의) 기적, 경적; 휘파람 (소리)
When someone whistles, they make a sound by forcing their breath out between their lips or their teeth.

murmur*
[mɔ́:rmər]

v. 속삭이다, 소곤거리다, 중얼거리다; n. 속삭임, 소곤거림
If you murmur something, you say it very quietly, so that not many people can hear what you are saying.

admiring
[ædmáiəriŋ]

a. 감탄하는, 찬양하는 (admiringly ad. 감탄하여)
An admiring expression shows that you like or respect someone or something.

assemble*
[əsémbl]

v. 모이다, 집합시키다; 조립하다
When people assemble or when someone assembles them, they come together in a group, usually for a particular purpose such as a meeting.

exhibit**
[igzíbit]

v. 전시하다; 보이다, 드러내다; n. 전시품 (exhibition n. 전시)
An exhibition is a public event at which pictures, sculptures, or other objects of interest are displayed, for example at a museum or art gallery.

submit*
[səbmít]

v. 제출하다; 항복하다, 굴복하다
If you submit a proposal, report, or request to someone, you formally send it to them so that they can consider it or decide about it.

opinion**
[əpínjən]

n 의견, 견해
Your opinion about something is what you think or believe about it.

judge[***]
[dʒʌdʒ]

n. 심판, 심사위원; 판사; v. 판단하다; 판정하다
A judge is a person who decides who will be the winner of a competition.

worthy[*]
[wɔ́:rði]

a. ~을 받을 만한, 자격이 있는; 훌륭한
If a person or thing is worthy of something, they deserve it because they have the qualities or abilities required.

unfortunate[*]
[ʌnfɔ́:rtʃənət]

a. 운이 없는, 불운한, 불행한 (unfortunately ad. 불행하게도, 유감스럽게도)
If you describe someone as unfortunate, you mean that something unpleasant or unlucky has happened to them.

absent[복습]
[ǽbsənt]

a. 결석한; 없는, 부재한; 멍한; v. 결석하다, 불참하다
If someone or something is absent from a place or situation where they should be or where they usually are, they are not there.

applause[*]
[əplɔ́:z]

n. 박수 (갈채)
Applause is the noise made by a group of people clapping their hands to show approval.

due[***]
[dju:]

a. (권리나 자격이 있는 사람에게) 주어야 하는; ~할 예정인; ~때문에, 덕분에
Something that is due, or that is due to someone, is owed to them, either as a debt or because they have a right to it.

file[*]
[fail]

v. 줄지어 가다; (소송 등을) 제기하다; (문서 등을) 보관하다; n. 파일, 서류철; 정보
When a group of people files somewhere, they walk one behind the other in a line.

exquisite
[ékskwizit]

a. 매우 아름다운, 정교한
Something that is exquisite is extremely beautiful or pleasant, especially in a delicate way.

burst into[복습]

idiom (갑자기) ~을 터뜨리다
If you burst into something, you start producing or doing it suddenly and with great force.

stamp[**]
[stæmp]

v. (발을) 구르다; (도장 · 스탬프 등을) 찍다; n. 우표; 도장
If you stamp or stamp your foot, you lift your foot and put it down very hard on the ground, for example because you are angry or because your feet are cold.

whisper[*]
[hwíspər]

v. 속삭이다, 소곤거리다; 은밀히 말하다; n. 속삭임, 소곤거리는 소리
When you whisper, you say something very quietly, using your breath rather than your throat, so that only one person can hear you.

monitor[*]
[mánətər]

n. 반장, 학급 요원; 감시 장치, 모니터; v. 감시하다; 추적 관찰하다
A monitor is a school student with disciplinary or other special duties.

principal[복습]
[prínsəpəl]

n. 교장; a. 주요한, 주된
The principal of a school or college is the person in charge of the school or college.

clap[*]
[klæp]

v. 박수를 치다; (갑자기 · 재빨리) 놓다; n. 박수; 쿵 하는 소리
When you clap, you hit your hands together to show appreciation or attract attention.

thoughtful*
[θɔ́:tfəl]

a. (조용히) 생각에 잠긴; 배려심 있는, 친절한 (thoughtfully ad. 생각에 잠겨)
If you are thoughtful, you are quiet and serious because you are thinking about something.

attention^{복습}
[əténʃən]

v. 알립니다, 주목하세요; n. 관심, 흥미; 주의, 주목
If you pay attention to someone, you watch them, listen to them, or take notice of them.

shuffle
[ʃʌfl]

v. 발을 끌며 걷다; (위치 · 순서를) 이리저리 바꾸다; n. 발을 끌며 걷기
If you shuffle somewhere, you walk there without lifting your feet properly off the ground.

tense**
[tens]

a. 긴장한, 신경이 날카로운; v. 긴장하다
A tense situation or period of time is one that makes people anxious, because they do not know what is going to happen next.

expectant
[ikspéktənt]

a. 기대하는
If someone is expectant, they are excited because they think something interesting is about to happen.

adjust**
[ədʒʌ́st]

v. (매무새 등을) 바로잡다; 조정하다, 조절하다; 적응하다
If you adjust something such as your clothing or a machine, you correct or alter its position or setting.

deliberate*
[dilíbərət]

a. 신중한, 계획적인 (deliberately ad. 신중하게, 계획적으로)
If a movement or action is deliberate, it is done slowly and carefully.

manner^{복습}
[mǽnər]

n. (사람의) 태도; (일의) 방식; (사회 · 문화적인) 예의
Someone's manner is the way in which they behave and talk when they are with other people, for example whether they are polite, confident, or bad-tempered.

indicate*
[índikèit]

v. 나타내다, 보여 주다; (손가락이나 고갯짓으로) 가리키다
If you indicate an opinion, an intention, or a fact, you mention it in an indirect way.

brief*
[bri:f]

a. (말 · 글이) 간단한; 짧은, 잠시 동안의
A brief speech or piece of writing does not contain too many words or details.

holler
[hálər]

v. 소리지르다, 고함치다
If you holler, you shout loudly.

wipe*
[waip]

v. (먼지 · 물기 등을) 닦다; 지우다; n. (행주 · 걸레를 써서) 닦기
If you wipe dirt or liquid from something, you remove it, for example by using a cloth or your hand.

handkerchief**
[hǽŋkərʧif]

n. 손수건
A handkerchief is a small square piece of fabric which you use for blowing your nose.

purposely
[pɔ́:rpəsli]

ad. 고의로, 일부러
If you do something purposely, you do it intentionally.

unfamiliar*
[ʌnfəmíljər]

a. 익숙하지 않은, 낯선; 지식이 없는, 잘 모르는
If something is unfamiliar to you, you know nothing or very little about it, because you have not seen or experienced it before.

prefer[**]
[prifə́:r]

v. (다른 것보다) ~을 (더) 좋아하다, 선호하다
If you prefer someone or something, you like that person or thing better than another, and so you are more likely to choose them if there is a choice.

thoughtless
[θɔ́:tlis]

a. 무심한, 배려심 없는 (thoughtlessness n. 생각이 모자람)
If you describe someone as thoughtless, you are critical of them because they forget or ignore other people's wants, needs, or feelings.

period[**]
[pí:əriəd]

n. (학교의 일과를 나눠 놓은) 시간; 기간, 시기; 마침표
At a school or college, a period is one of the parts that the day is divided into during which lessons or other activities take place.

put one's mind on

idiom ~에 집중하다, ~에 열중하다
If you put your mind on something or set your mind on it, you are determined to do it or obtain it.

stomach[**]
[stʌ́mək]

n. 복부, 배, 속
(in the bottom of one's stomach idiom (강한 감정을 나타낼 때) 마음속에서)
You can use unfortunately to introduce or refer to a statement when you consider that it is sad or disappointing, or when you want to express regret.

closet[복습]
[klázit]

n. 벽장
A closet is a piece of furniture with doors at the front and shelves inside, which is used for storing things.

stand by

idiom (방관·좌시하며) 가만히 있다
If you stand by, you allow something unpleasant to happen without doing anything to stop it.

coward[*]
[káuərd]

n. 겁쟁이, 비겁자
If you call someone a coward, you disapprove of them because they are easily frightened and avoid dangerous or difficult situations.

mean[**]
[mi:n]

a. (사람·행동이) 못된, 심술궂은; 별로 뛰어나지 못한
If someone is being mean, they are being unkind to another person, for example by not allowing them to do something.

make fun of[복습]

idiom ~을 놀리다
If you make fun of someone or something you laugh at them, tease them, or make jokes about them in a way that causes them to seem ridiculous.

put oneself in a person's shoes

idiom 남의 입장이 되어 생각하다
If you put yourself in someone's shoes, you imagine what it is like to be in their position.

miserable[*]
[mízərəbl]

a. 비참한; 우울하게 만드는; 보잘것없는
If you are miserable, you are very unhappy.

goodness[복습]
[gúdnis]

int. 와!, 어머나!, 맙소사!; n. 신; 선량함
People sometimes say 'goodness' or 'my goodness' to express surprise.

48

steal***
[sti:l]

v. (stole–stolen) 살며시 움직이다; 훔치다, 도둑질하다
(steal a glance **idiom** 몰래 훔쳐보다)
If someone steals somewhere, they move there quietly, in a secret way.

glance*
[glæns]

n. 흘낏 봄; v. 흘낏 보다; 대충 훑어보다 (steal a glance **idiom** 몰래 훔쳐보다)
If you steal a glance at someone or something, you look at them quickly so that nobody sees you looking.

dismiss**
[dismís]

v. (사람을) 해산시키다; 묵살하다; (생각 · 느낌을) 떨쳐 버리다
If you are dismissed by someone in authority, they tell you that you can go away from them.

pretend^{복습}
[priténd]

v. ~인 척하다, ~인 것처럼 굴다; ~라고 가장하다 (pretended a. 거짓의)
If something is pretended, it is not genuine or sincere.

casual**
[kǽʒuəl]

a. 태평스러운 (듯한), 무심한; 격식을 차리지 않는, 평상시의
(casualness n. 태평스러움)
If you are casual, you are, or you pretend to be, relaxed and not very concerned about what is happening or what you are doing.

glow*
[glou]

v. (기쁨 · 만족감에 얼굴 등이) 빛나다; 빛나다, 타다; (얼굴이) 상기되다;
n. (은은한) 불빛; 홍조
If someone glows with an emotion such as pride or pleasure, the expression on their face shows how they feel.

chapter six

1. Why did Maddie hope they would find Wanda?
   A. She wanted to ask about her dresses one last time.
   B. She wanted to ask Wanda to draw a picture of her wearing a dress.
   C. She wanted to give Wanda her medal before she moved away.
   D. She wanted to apologize and tell her that people would be nice.

2. How did Maddie imagine her and Peggy helping Wanda?
   A. Maddie imagined them buying Wanda new dresses for school.
   B. Maddie imagined them fighting anyone who was not nice to Wanda.
   C. Maddie imagined them all drawing dresses together at Wanda's house.
   D. Maddie imagined them walking with her and Jake to school each morning.

3. How did Wanda's house remind Maddie of Wanda's dress?
   A. It was Polish.
   B. It was faded blue.
   C. It looked warm.
   D. It was shabby but clean.

4. How did the girls react to Mr. Svenson?
   A. Maddie covered her nose because she thought he smelled bad.
   B. They stayed to talk with him about his life on Boggins Heights.

50

C. Peggy yelled asking if he knew when the Petronskis moved and they ran away.

D. They asked him if he knew where Wanda had moved as they passed by him.

5. Which of the following was NOT a way that Maddie thought she could contact Wanda?

A. She thought that the teacher might know where she moved.

B. She thought that Mr. Svenson might know where she moved.

C. She thought that the post office might know where she moved.

D. She thought that she could go to the big city and find Wanda.

6. How did Peggy feel about teasing Wanda about the dresses?

A. She felt that her teasing helped Wanda think of ideas for drawing.

B. She felt bad that she didn't have the chance to apologize directly.

C. She felt bad for losing the drawing and color contest to Wanda.

D. She felt that her teasing helped Wanda make more friends in the big city.

7. What did Maddie finally decide after she felt that she could never make things right with Wanda?

A. She decided to never stand by and say nothing again.

B. She decided to start bullying other students in order to become popular.

C. She decided to move away from her school to live in the big city and visit Wanda.

D. She decided to do whatever it took to keep being friends with Peggy.

1분에 몇 단어를 읽는지 리딩 속도를 측정해보세요.

$$\frac{1{,}395 \text{ words}}{\text{reading time ( ) sec}} \times 60 = (\quad) \text{ WPM}$$

Build Your Vocabulary

height^{복습}
[hait]

n. 높은 곳; (사물의) 높이; (사람의) 키
A height is a high position or place above the ground.

forbidding
[fərbídiŋ]

a. 험악한, 으스스한
If you describe a person, place, or thing as forbidding, you mean they have a severe, unfriendly, or threatening appearance.

drizzle^{복습}
[drizl]

n. 이슬비, 가랑비; v. (비가) 보슬보슬 내리다; (액체를) 조금 붓다
(drizzly a. 이슬비가 내리는)
When the weather is drizzly, the sky is dull and grey and it rains steadily but not very hard.

damp[*]
[dæmp]

a. 축축한; n. 습기
Something that is damp is slightly wet.

dismal[*]
[dízməl]

a. 음울한, 울적하게 하는; 형편없는
Something that is dismal is sad and depressing, especially in appearance.

gruff
[grʌf]

a. (행동이) 거친; (목소리가) 걸걸한 (gruffly ad. 무뚝뚝하게)
If you describe someone as gruff, you mean that they seem rather unfriendly or bad-tempered.

foreigner[*]
[fɔ́:rənər]

n. 외국인
A foreigner is someone who belongs to a country that is not your own.

make fun of^{복습}

idiom ~을 놀리다
If you make fun of someone or something, you laugh at them, tease them, or make jokes about them in a way that causes them to seem ridiculous.

sense^{복습}
[sens]

n. 지각, 일리; 감각; v. 감지하다, 느끼다
Sense is the ability to make good judgments and to behave sensibly.

dumb^{복습}
[dʌm]

a. 멍청한, 바보 같은; 말을 못 하는
If you say that something is dumb, you think that it is silly and annoying.

pick on

idiom (부당하게) ~을 괴롭히다
If you pick on someone, you treat them badly or unfairly, especially repeatedly.

assail
[əséil]

v. 공격을 가하다; (몹시) 괴롭히다
If someone assails you, they criticize you strongly.

52

bully^{복습}
[búli]

n. (약자를) 괴롭히는 사람; v. (약자를) 괴롭히다; 협박하다
A bully is someone who uses their strength or power to hurt or frighten other people.

yell^{복습}
[jel]

v. 소리치다, 소리 지르다, 외치다; n. 고함, 외침
If you yell, you shout loudly, usually because you are excited, angry, or in pain.

pounce
[pauns]

v. (공격하거나 잡으려고 확) 덮치다, 덤비다
If someone pounces on you, they come up toward you suddenly and take hold of you.

guilty**
[gílti]

a. (잘못된 ㄹ에 대해) 책임이 있는; 죄책감이 드는, 가책을 느끼는
If someone is guilty of doing something wrong, they have done that thing.

console*
[kənsóul]

① v. 위로하다, 위안을 주다 ② n. 콘솔, 제어반, 계기반
If you console someone who is unhappy about something, you try to make them feel more cheerful.

vanish*
[vǽniʃ]

v. 사라지다, 없어지다; 모습을 감추다
If someone or something vanishes, they disappear suddenly or in a way that cannot be explained.

drab
[dræb]

a. 생기 없는, 칙칙한; 재미없는
If you describe something as drab, you think that it is dull and boring to look at or experience.

cheerless
[tʃíərlis]

a. 생기 없는, 칙칙한
Cheerless places or weather are dull and depressing.

sumac
[ʃú:mæk]

n. 옻나무
A sumac is a shrub or small tree with compound leaves, reddish hairy fruits in conical clusters, and bright autumn colors.

fern*
[fə:rn]

n. 양치식물
A fern is a plant that has long stems with feathery leaves and no flowers.

brook*
[bruk]

① n. 시내, 개천 ② v. 견디다, 참다
A brook is a small stream.

lush
[lʌʃ]

a. (식물 · 정원 등이) 무성한, 우거진; 멋진
Lush fields or gardens have a lot of very healthy grass or plants.

shrink*
[ʃriŋk]

v. (shrank–shrunk) (규모 · 양이) 줄어들다; (놀람 · 충격으로) 움츠러들다
If something shrinks or something else shrinks it, it becomes smaller.

mere**
[míər]

a. (merest) 겨우 ~의, 한낱 ~에 불과한
You use mere to emphasize how small a particular amount or number is.

trickle
[tríkl]

n. 조금씩 흐르는 소량의 액체; v. (액체가 가늘게) 흐르다; 천천히 흘러가다
Trickle is a small amount of a liquid or other substance that flows slowly.

sharpen^{복습}
[ʃáːrpən]

v. 선명해지다, 날카로워지다; (날카롭게) 갈다, 깎다
If your senses, understanding, or skills sharpen or are sharpened, you become better at noticing things, thinking, or doing something.

outline*
[áutlàin]

n. 윤곽; 개요; v. 개요를 서술하다; 윤곽을 보여주다
The outline of something is its general shape, especially when it cannot be clearly seen.

rusty^{복습}
[rʌ́sti]

a. 녹슨, 녹 투성이의; 예전 같지 않은
A rusty metal object such as a car or a machine is covered with rust, which is a brown substance that forms on iron or steel when it comes into contact with water.

tin^{복습}
[tin]

n. 깡통; 통조림 (tin can n. 빈 깡통)
A tin is a metal container which is filled with food and sealed in order to preserve the food for long periods of time.

forlorn*
[fəːrlɔ́ːrn]

a. 황량한, 버려진; 쓸쓸해 보이는; 허망한
Forlorn means pitifully sad and abandoned or lonely.

remnant
[rémnənt]

n. (pl.) 남은 부분, 나머지; 자투리(천)
The remnants of something are small parts of it that are left over when the main part has disappeared or been destroyed.

bed***
[bed]

n. (강·바다 등의) 바닥; 침대
The sea bed or a river bed is the ground at the bottom of the sea or of a river.

otherwise**
[ʌ́ðərwàiz]

ad. 그렇지 않으면; 그 외에는
You use otherwise after stating a situation or fact, in order to say what the result or consequence would be if this situation or fact was not the case.

puff*
[pʌf]

v. 숨을 헐떡거리다; (담배·파이프 등을) 뻐끔뻐끔 피우다; (연기·김을) 내뿜다; n. 부푼 것; (담배·파이프 등을) 피우기
If you are puffing, you are breathing loudly and quickly with your mouth open because you are out of breath after a lot of physical effort.

pant*
[pænt]

v. (숨을) 헐떡이다; n. 헐떡거림
If you pant, you breathe quickly and loudly with your mouth open, because you have been doing something energetic.

round**
[raund]

v. (모퉁이·커브 등을) 돌다; 둥글게 만들다; ad. 여기저기, 도처에; n. 회진, 순찰; 한 차례
If you round a place or obstacle, you move in a curve past the edge or corner of it.

rickety
[ríkiti]

a. 곧 무너질 듯한, 부서질 듯한
A rickety structure or piece of furniture is not very strong or well made, and seems likely to collapse or break.

tiptoe
[típtòu]

n. 발끝; v. (발끝으로) 살금살금 걷다 (on tiptoe idiom 발끝으로)
If you do something on tiptoe or on tiptoes, you do it standing or walking on the front part of your foot, without putting your heels on the ground.

54

nonsense**
[nánsens]

n. 터무니없는 생각, 허튼소리
If you say that something spoken or written is nonsense, you mean that you consider it to be untrue or silly.

flea*
[fli:]

n. 벼룩
A flea is a very small jumping insect that has no wings and feeds on the blood of humans or animals.

customary*
[kʌ́stəmèri]

a. 습관적인; 관례적인, 관습상의
Customary is used to describe something that a particular person usually does or has.

tilt^{복습}
[tilt]

v. 기울다, (뒤로) 젖혀지다; (의견 · 상황 등이) 기울어지다; n. 기울어짐, 젖혀짐
If you tilt an object or if it tilts, it moves into a sloping position with one end or side higher than the other.

spit*
[spit]

v. (침 · 음식 등을) 뱉다; (탁탁거리며) 뱉다; n. 침; 뱉기
If you spit liquid or food somewhere, you force a small amount of it out of your mouth.

sight**
[sait]

n. 시야; 시력; 광경, 모습 (in sight idiom ~이 보이는 곳에)
If something is in sight or within sight, you can see it.

bark*
[ba:rk]

v. (개가) 짖다; (명령 · 질문 등을) 빽 내지르다; n. (개 등이) 짖는 소리; 나무껍질
When a dog barks, it makes a short, loud noise, once or several times.

coop
[ku:p]

n. 닭장, (짐승의) 우리
A coop is a cage where you keep small animals or birds such as chickens and rabbits.

wisp
[wisp]

n. (작고 가느다란 것의) 조각, 가닥; (연기 · 구름의) 줄기
A wisp of hair is a small, thin, untidy bunch of it.

stick**
[stik]

v. (stuck-stuck) 내밀다; 찌르다, 박다; 달라붙다; 집어넣다; n. 나뭇가지
If something sticks up, it points upward.

pathway
[pǽθwèi]

n. (사람만이 다닐 수 있는) 좁은 길, 오솔길
A pathway is a path which you can walk along or a route which you can take.

kitten*
[kitn]

n. 새끼 고양이
A kitten is a very young cat.

sparse
[spa:rs]

a. 드문, (밀도가) 희박한
Something that is sparse is small in number or amount and spread out over an area.

yard^{복습}
[ja:rd]

n. 마당, 뜰; (학교의) 운동장; 정원
A yard is a piece of land next to someone's house, with grass and plants growing in it.

shabby*
[ʃǽbi]

a. 허름한, 다 낡은, 해진
Shabby things or places look old and in bad condition.

fade^{복습}
[feid]

v. (색깔이) 바래다, 희미해지다; 서서히 사라지다, 점점 희미해지다
(faded a. 빛깔이 바랜)
When a colored object fades or when the light fades it, it gradually becomes paler.

except^{복습}
[iksépt]

prep. (누구 · 무엇을) 제외하고는
You use except to introduce the only thing or person that a statement does not apply to, or a fact that prevents a statement from being completely true.

crouch[*]
[krauʧ]

v. (몸을) 쭈그리다, 쭈그리고 앉다; n. 쭈그리고 앉기
If you are crouching, your legs are bent under you so that you are close to the ground and leaning forward slightly.

leap[*]
[li:p]

v. (leaped/leapt–leaped/leapt) 뛰다, 뛰어오르다; (서둘러) ~하다;
n. 높이뛰기, 도약; 급증
If you leap, you jump high in the air or jump a long distance.

timid^{복습}
[tímid]

a. 소심한, 자신감이 없는 (timidly ad. 소심하게)
Timid people are shy, nervous, and have no courage or confidence in themselves.

halfway[*]
[hǽfwèi]

ad. (거리 · 시간상으로) 중간에
Halfway means in the middle of a place or between two points, at an equal distance from each of them.

knock^{**}
[nak]

v. (문 등을 똑똑 하고) 두드리다; 치다, 찧다; n. 문 두드리는 소리
If you knock on something such as a door or window, you hit it, usually several times, to attract someone's attention.

firm^{복습}
[fə:rm]

a. 단호한, 단단한; 딱딱한; 확고한; n. 회사 (firmly ad. 단호히)
If you describe someone as firm, you mean they behave in a way that shows that they are not going to change their mind, or that they are the person who is in control.

backyard[*]
[bæ̀kjá:rd]

n. 뒤뜰
A backyard is an area of land at the back of a house.

eardrum
[íərdrʌm]

n. 고막
Your eardrums are the thin pieces of tightly stretched skin inside each ear, which vibrate when sound waves reach them.

furniture^{**}
[fə́:rniʧər]

n. 가구
Furniture consists of large objects such as tables, chairs, or beds that are used in a room for sitting or lying on or for putting things on or in.

suggest^{복습}
[səgdʒést]

v. 말하다, (뜻을) 비치다; (아이디어 · 계획을) 제안하다; 추천하다
If you suggest that something is the case, you say something which you believe is the case.

hopeful^{**}
[hóupfəl]

a. 희망에 찬, 기대하는 (hopefully ad. 희망을 갖고)
If you are hopeful, you are fairly confident that something that you want to happen will happen.

bear^{**}
[bɛər]

v. 참다, 견디다; (책임 등을) 떠맡다, 감당하다; (아이를) 낳다; n. 곰
If you bear an unpleasant experience, you accept it because you are unable to do anything about it.

hard fact
[há:rd fækt]

n. 확실한 정보; 엄연한 사실
The hard fact means information that is definitely true and can be proved.

amend[*]
[əménd]

v. 고치다, 수정하다 (make amends idiom 보상해 주다)
If you make amends when you have harmed someone, you show that you are sorry by doing something to please them.

cautious[*]
[kɔ́:ʃəs]

a. 조심스러운, 신중한 (cautiously ad. 조심스럽게)
If you describe someone's attitude or reaction as cautious, you mean that it is limited or careful.

knob[*]
[nab]

n. (동그란) 손잡이; 혹, 마디
A knob is a round handle on a door or drawer which you use in order to open or close it.

furnish[*]
[fə́:rniʃ]

v. (가구를) 비치하다; 공급하다, 제공하다
If you furnish a room or building, you put furniture and furnishings into it.

frail[*]
[freil]

a. 허약한, 부서지기 쉬운; 노쇠한
Something that is frail is easily broken or damaged.

absolute[*]
[ǽbsəlù:t]

a. 완전한, 완벽한 (absolutely ad. 전혀; 전적으로, 틀림없이)
Absolutely means totally and completely.

imaginary[**]
[imǽdʒənèri]

a. 상상에만 존재하는, 가상적인
An imaginary person, place, or thing exists only in your mind or in a story, and not in real life.

forward[복습]
[fɔ́:rwərd]

v. (이사 간 사람에게 배달된 편지 등을 새 주소로) 다시 보내 주다; 전달하다; ad. 앞으로; 더 일찍
If a letter or message is forwarded to someone, it is sent to the place where they are, after having been sent to a different place earlier.

downcast
[dáunkæst]

a. 풀이 죽은; (눈을) 내리뜬
If you are downcast, you are feeling sad and without hope.

discourage[*]
[diskə́:ridʒ]

v. 의욕을 꺾다, 좌절시키다; (무엇을 어렵게 만들거나 반대하여) 막다 (discouraged a. 낙담한, 낙심한)
If someone or something discourages you, they cause you to lose your enthusiasm about your actions.

distance[**]
[dístəns]

n. 먼 곳; 거리; v. (~에) 관여하지 않다 (in the distance idiom 저 멀리, 먼 곳에)
If you can see something in the distance, you can see it, far away from you but still able to be seen or heard.

bay[복습]
[bei]

n. 만(灣); 구역, 구간; 월계수 잎
A bay is a part of a coast where the land curves inward.

bend[**]
[bend]

n. (도로 · 강의) 굽이, 굽은 곳; v. (몸 · 머리를) 굽히다, 숙이다; 구부리다
A bend in a road, pipe, or other long thin object is a curve or angle in it.

dilapidated
[dilǽpədèitid]

a. 다 허물어져 가는
A building that is dilapidated is old and in a generally bad condition.

goodness[복습]
[gúdnis]

int. 와!, 어머나!, 맙소사!; n. 신; 선량함
People sometimes say 'goodness' or 'my goodness' to express surprise.

chapter six

57

trousers*
[tráuzərz]

n. (남자용) 바지
Trousers are a piece of clothing that you wear over your body from the waist downward, and that cover each leg separately.

droop*
[dru:p]

v. 아래로 처지다; 풀이 죽다, (기가) 꺾이다
If something droops, it hangs or leans downward with no strength or firmness.

mustache*
[mʌ́stæʃ]

n. 콧수염
A man's mustache is the hair that grows on his upper lip.

tangle*
[tæŋgl]

v. 헝클어지다, 얽히다; n. (실ㆍ머리카락 등이) 엉킨 것; (혼란스럽게) 꼬인 상태
(tangled a. 헝클어진)
If something is tangled or tangles, it becomes twisted together in an untidy way.

hound*
[haund]

n. 사냥개; v. 따라다니며 괴롭히다
A hound is a type of dog that is often used for hunting or racing.

lope
[loup]

v. 천천히 달리다
If a person or animal lopes somewhere, they run in an easy and relaxed way, taking long steps.

stream**
[stri:m]

n. (액체ㆍ기체의) 줄기; 개울, 시내; v. (액체ㆍ기체가) 줄줄 흐르다
A stream of smoke, air, or liquid is a narrow moving mass of it.

expert*
[ékspə:rt]

a. 숙련된; 전문가의, 전문적인; n. 전문가 (expertly ad. 훌륭하게, 전문적으로)
Someone who is expert at doing something is very skilled at it.

scatter*복습
[skǽtər]

v. 흩뿌리다; 황급히 흩어지다; n. 흩뿌리기; 소수, 소량 (scattered a. 드문드문 있는)
Scattered things are spread over an area in an untidy or irregular way.

path**
[pæθ]

n. 길; 방향; 계획
A path is a long strip of ground which people walk along to get from one place to another.

intelligible
[intélədʒəbl]

a. (쉽게) 이해할 수 있는 (unintelligible a. 이해할 수 없는)
Unintelligible language is impossible to understand, for example because it is not written or pronounced clearly, or because its meaning is confused or complicated.

mutter*
[mʌ́tər]

v. 중얼거리다; 투덜거리다; n. 중얼거림
If you mutter, you speak very quietly so that you cannot easily be heard, often because you are complaining about something.

scratch*
[skrætʃ]

v. 긁다; 할퀴다; n. 긁힌 자국, 찰과상
If you scratch yourself, you rub your fingernails against your skin because it is itching.

disconsolate
[diskánsələt]

a. 암담한
Someone who is disconsolate is very unhappy and depressed.

slide*복습
[slaid]

v. 미끄러지다; 슬며시 움직이다; n. 떨어짐; 미끄러짐
When something slides somewhere or when you slide it there, it moves there smoothly over or against something.

58

bump[*]
[bʌmp]

v. (~에) 부딪치다; 덜컹거리며 가다; n. 부딪치기, 충돌; 쿵 (하고 부딪치는 소리)
If you bump into something or someone, you accidentally hit them while you are moving.

smack[*]
[smæk]

ad. 정통으로; v. 탁 소리가 나게 치다; n. 탁 (하는 소리)
Something that is smack in a particular place is exactly in that place.

besides[복습]
[bisáidz]

ad. 게다가, 뿐만 아니라; prep. ~외에
Besides is used to emphasize an additional point that you are making, especially one that you consider to be important.

turn over

idiom ~을 곰곰이 생각하다
To turn over something means to think carefully about all the details of it.

glow[복습]
[glou]

v. 빛나다, 타다; (기쁨·만족감에 얼굴 등이) 빛나다; (얼굴이) 상기되다;
n. (은은한) 불빛; 홍조
If a place glows with a color or a quality, it is bright, attractive, and colorful.

forehead[복습]
[fɔ́:rhèd]

n. 이마
Your forehead is the area at the front of your head between your eyebrows and your hair.

conclusion[*]
[kənklú:ʒən]

n. 결론, (최종적인) 판단
When you come to a conclusion, you decide that something is true after you have thought about it carefully and have considered all the relevant facts.

stand by[복습]

idiom (방관·좌시하며) 가만히 있다
If you stand by, you allow something unpleasant to happen without doing anything to stop it.

speak up

idiom (~을 지지한다는 뜻을) 거리낌 없이 말하다
If you speak you for someone or something, you say what you think clearly and freely, especially to support or defend them.

friendship[*]
[fréndʃip]

n. 교우 관계; 우정; 친선
A friendship is a relationship between two or more friends.

chapter seven

1. What kind of letter did Maddie and Peggy want to write
    to Wanda?
    A. They wanted to write that they were sorry.
    B. They wanted to write just a friendly letter.
    C. They wanted to write a a letter congratulating her for winning the
        contest.
    D. They wanted to write a letter to invite her back to their school.

2. How Maddie and Peggy feel immediately after they mailed
    the letter?
    A. They both felt bad for her not having parents.
    B. They both felt happier and more carefree.
    C. They both decided to write another letter of apology.
    D. They both were worried that she would not get the letter.

3. What surprise did Miss Mason have for Room 13 at the
    Christmas party?
    A. Jack Beggles had dressed up like Santa Claus.
    B. Miss Mason had baked them all fresh cookies.
    C. Miss Mason read a letter from Wanda.
    D. Wanda came back to visit the class.

4. How did Wanda feel about the drawings of the dresses that she left behind?

   A. She wanted them all to be thrown away.

   B. She wanted Miss Mason to mail them all back to her.

   C. She wanted them to be kept up in the classroom all year long.

   D. She wanted them to be shared in the class with special ones for Peggy and Maddie.

5. How did Peggy feel about the letter from Wanda?

   A. She felt bad that she would never see Wanda again.

   B. She felt bad that she couldn't ever really make things right between them.

   C. She felt that the letter was Wanda's way of saying that everything's all right.

   D. She felt that Wanda had never received the letter that they had sent to her.

6. Why was Maddie so excited that she ran to Peggy's house?

   A. Maddie had received a letter from Wanda that she wanted to share.

   B. Maddie noticed that the face and the hair in the drawing looked like herself.

   C. Maddie wanted to draw a dress for Wanda and send it to her as a present.

   D. Maddie had received a real dress that looked just like Wanda's drawing.

7. Why did Peggy and Maddie feel that Wanda must have liked them after all?

   A. Wanda had sent them Christmas presents.

   B. Wanda had called them her best friends.

   C. Wanda had come back to the school.

   D. Wanda had drawn both Peggy and Maddie.

$$\frac{1{,}233 \text{ words}}{\text{reading time ( ) sec}} \times 60 = (\quad) \text{ WPM}$$

Build Your Vocabulary

friendly**
[fréndli]

a. (행동이) 친절한; 상냥한, 다정한
If someone is friendly, they behave in a pleasant, kind way, and like to be with other people.

contest 복습
[kántest]

n. 대회, 시합
A contest is a competition or game in which people try to win.

forward 복습
[fɔ́:rwərd]

v. (이사 간 사람에게 배달된 편지 등을 새 주소로) 다시 보내 주다; 전달하다;
ad. 앞으로; 더 일찍
If a letter or message is forwarded to someone, it is sent to the place where they are, after having been sent to a different place earlier.

envelope*
[énvəlòup]

n. 봉투
An envelope is the rectangular paper cover in which you send a letter to someone through the post.

mailbox*
[méilbaks]

n. 우체통
A mailbox is a metal box in a public place, where you put letters and packets to be collected.

carefree
[kéərfri:]

a. 근심 걱정 없는, 속 편한
A carefree person or period of time doesn't have or involve any problems, worries, or responsibilities.

blame**
[bleim]

v. ~을 탓하다, ~의 책임으로 보다; n. 책임; 탓
If you blame a person or thing for something bad, you believe or say that they are responsible for it or that they caused it.

hitch 복습
[hitʃ]

v. (위로) 몸을 올리다; (지나가는 차를) 얻어 타다
If you hitch a part of your body or something that you are carrying, you move it to a higher position.

queer*
[kwiər]

a. 별난, 기묘한, 이상한
Something that is queer is strange.

lace*
[leis]

v. 끈으로 묶다; 가미하다; 첨가되다; n. (구두 등의) 끈, 엮은 끈
(laced a. 끈이 달린, 끈으로 졸라맨)
If you lace something such as a pair of shoes, you tighten the shoes by pulling the laces through the holes, andusually tying them together.

iron 복습
[áiərn]

v. 다리미질을 하다; n. 철, 쇠
If you iron clothes, you remove the creases from them using an iron.

overnight*
[òuvərnáit]

ad. 밤사이에, 하룻밤 동안; a. 야간의; 하룻밤 동안의
If something happens overnight, it happens throughout the night or at some point during the night.

tease^{복습}
[ti:z]

v. 놀리다, 장난하다; (동물을) 못 살게 굴다; n. 장난, 놀림
To tease someone means to laugh at them or make jokes about them in order to embarrass, annoy, or upset them.

ashamed**
[əʃéimd]

a. (~여서) 부끄러운, 창피한
If someone is ashamed, they feel embarrassed or guilty because of something they do or they have done, or because of their appearance.

rescue*
[réskju:]

v. 구하다, 구출하다; n. 구출, 구조, 구제
If you rescue someone, you get them out of a dangerous or unpleasant situation.

sink^{복습}
[siŋk]

v. 가라앉다, 빠지다; (양·강도 등이) 약해지다; n. (부엌의) 싱크대, 개수대
If a boat sinks or if someone or something sinks it, it disappears below the surface of a mass of water.

hoof*
[huf]

n. 발굽; 발굽 소리
The hoofs of an animal such as a horse are the hard lower parts of its feet.

runaway
[rʌ́nəwei]

a. (동물이) 고삐 풀린; 달아난, 가출한; n. 도망자
A runaway vehicle or animal is moving forward quickly, and its driver or rider has lost control of it.

dull^{복습}
[dʌl]

a. 무딘; 둔한; 흐릿한; 따분한, 재미없는
Dull feelings are weak and not intense.

pained
[peind]

a. 짜증스러워 하는, 화난
If you have a pained expression or look, you look upset, worried, or slightly annoyed.

decorate**
[dékərèit]

v. 장식하다, 꾸미다
If you decorate something, you make it more attractive by adding things to it.

blackboard^{복습}
[blǽkbɔ̀:rd]

n. 칠판
A blackboard is a dark-colored board that you can write on with chalk.

jolly^{복습}
[dʒáli]

a. 행복한, 쾌활한; 즐거운
Someone who is jolly is happy and cheerful in their appearance or behavior.

chalk^{복습}
[tʃɔ:k]

n. 분필
Chalk is small sticks of soft white rock, used for writing or drawing with.

costume*
[kástju:m]

n. 의상, 복장
An actor's or performer's costume is the set of clothes they wear while they are performing.

gaze[*]
[geiz]

v. (가만히) 응시하다, 바라보다; n. 응시, (눈여겨보는) 시선
If you gaze at someone or something, you look steadily at them for a long time.

hasty[*]
[héisti]

a. 서두른; 성급한 (hastily ad. 급히, 서둘러서)
A hasty movement, action, or statement is sudden, and often done in reaction to something that has just happened.

rub^{**}
[rʌb]

v. (손·손수건 등을 대고) 문지르다; (두 손 등을) 맞비비다; n. 문지르기, 비비기
If you rub a part of your body, you move your hand or fingers backward and forward over it while pressing firmly.

vivid^{복습}
[vívid]

a. 선명한, 강렬한; 생생한
Something that is vivid is very bright in color.

scarcely[*]
[skέərsli]

ad. 겨우, 간신히; 거의 ~않다
You use scarcely to emphasize that something is only just true or only just the case.

notice^{복습}
[nóutis]

v. ~을 의식하다, 알다; 주목하다; n. 신경씀, 주목, 알아챔
If you notice something or someone, you become aware of them.

blond^{복습}
[bland]

a. (머리가) 금발인
Blond hair can be very light brown or light yellow.

clatter[*]
[klǽtər]

v. 달그락거리며 가다; 쨍그랑하는 소리를 내다
If you say that people or things clatter somewhere, you mean that they move there noisily.

facedown
[feisdáun]

ad. 겉을 아래로 하고; 얼굴을 숙이고
If you put something facedown, the surface or front is downward.

exclaim^{복습}
[ikskléim]

v. 소리치다, 외치다
If you exclaim, you cry out suddenly in surprise, strong emotion, or pain.

auburn^{복습}
[ɔ́:bərn]

a. 적갈색의, 황갈색의; n. (머리털 등의) 적갈색, 황갈색
Auburn hair is reddish brown.

blink^{복습}
[bliŋk]

v. 눈을 깜박이다; (불빛이) 깜박거리다; n. 눈을 깜박거림
(blink away idiom 눈을 깜박여 눈물을 참다)
If you blink away something such as tears, you try to control tears or clear your eyes by blinking.

spot^{복습}
[spat]

n. (특정한) 곳; (작은) 점; v. 발견하다, 찾다, 알아채다
You can refer to a particular place as a spot.

yard^{복습}
[jaːrd]

n. (학교의) 운동장; 마당, 뜰; 정원 (school yard n. 학교 운동장)
The school yard is the large open area with a hard surface just outside a school building, where the schoolchildren can play and do other activities.

stolid^{복습}
[stálid]

a. 둔감한, 무신경한 (stolidly ad. 둔감하게, 무신경하게)
If you describe someone as stolid, you mean that they do not show much emotion or are not very exciting or interesting.

66

수고하셨습니다!

드디어 끝까지 다 읽으셨군요! 축하드립니다! 여러분은 이 책을 통해 총 7,329개의 단어를 읽으셨고, 500개 이상의 어휘와 표현들을 익히셨습니다. 이 책에 나온 어휘는 다른 원서를 읽을 때에도 빈번히 만날 수 있는 필수 어휘들입니다. 이 책을 읽었던 경험은 비슷한 수준의 다른 원서들을 읽을 때 큰 도움이 될 것입니다. 이제 자신의 상황에 맞게 원서를 반복해서 읽거나, 오디오북을 들어 볼 수 있습니다. 혹은 비슷한 수준의 다른 원서를 찾아 읽는 것도 좋습니다. 일단 원서를 완독한 뒤에 어떻게 계속 영어 공부를 이어갈 수 있을지, 도움말을 꼼꼼히 살펴보고 각자 상황에 맞게 적용해 보세요!

리딩(Reading)을 확실하게 다지고 싶다면? 반복해서 읽어 보세요!

리딩 실력을 탄탄하게 다지고 싶다면, 같은 원서를 2~3번 반복해서 읽을 것을 권합니다. 같은 책을 여러 번 읽으면 지루할 것 같지만, 꼭 그렇지도 않습니다. 반복해서 읽을 때 처음과 주안점을 다르게 두면, 전혀 다른 느낌으로 재미있게 읽을 수 있습니다.

처음 원서를 읽을 때는 생소한 단어들과 스토리로 인해 읽으면서 곧바로 이해하기가 매우 힘들 수 있습니다. 전체 맥락을 잡고 읽어도 약간 버거운 느낌이지요. 하지만 반복해서 읽기 시작하면 달라집니다. 일단 내용을 파악한 상황이기 때문에 문장 구조나 어휘의 활용에 더 집중하게 되고, 조금 더 깊이 있게 읽을 수 있습니다. 좋은 표현과 문장을 수집하고 메모할 만한 여유도 생기게 되지요. 어휘도 많이 익숙해졌기 때문에 리딩 속도에도 탄력이 붙습니다. 처음 읽을 때는 '내용'에서 재미를 느꼈다면, 반복해서 읽을 때에는 '영어'에서 재미를 느끼게 되는 것입니다. 따라서 리딩 실력을 더욱 확고하게 다지고자 한다면, 같은 책을 2~3회 정도 반복해서 읽을 것을 권해 드립니다.

리스닝(Listening) 실력을 늘리고 싶다면?
귀를 통해서 읽어 보세요!

많은 영어 학습자들이 '리스닝이 안 돼서 문제'라고 한탄합니다. 그리고 리스닝 실력을 늘리는 방법으로 무슨 뜻인지 몰라도 반복해서 듣는 '무작정 듣기'를 선택합니다. 하지만 뜻도 모르면서 무작정 듣는 일에는 엄청난 인내력이 필요합니다. 그래서 대부분 며칠 시도하다가 포기해 버리고 말지요.

따라서 모르는 내용을 무작정 듣는 것보다는 어느 정도 알고 있는 내용을 반복해서 듣는 것이 더 효과적인 듣기 방법입니다. 그리고 이런 방식의 듣기에 활용할 수 있는 가장 좋은 교재가 오디오북입니다.

리스닝 실력을 향상하고 싶다면, 이 책에서 제공하는 오디오북을 이용해서 듣는 연습을 해 보세요. 활용법은 간단합니다. 일단 책을 한 번 완독했다면, 오디오북을 통해 다시 들어 보는 것입니다. 휴대 기기에 넣어 시간이 날 때 틈틈이 듣는 것도 좋고, 책상에 앉아 눈으로는 텍스트를 보며 귀로 읽는 것도 좋습니다. 이미 읽었던 내용이라 이해하기가 훨씬 수월하고, 애매했던 발음들도 자연스럽게 교정할 수 있습니다. 또 성우의 목소리 연기를 듣다 보면 내용이 더욱 생동감 있게 다가와 이해도가 높아지는 효과도 거둘 수 있습니다.

반대로 듣기에 자신 있는 사람이라면, 책을 읽기 전에 처음부터 오디오북을 먼저 듣는 것도 좋은 방법입니다. 귀를 통해 책을 쭉 읽어 보고, 이후에 다시 눈으로 책을 읽으면서 잘 들리지 않았던 부분을 보충하는 것이지요.

중요한 것은 내용을 따라가면서, 내용에 푹 빠져서 반복해 들어야 한다는 것입니다. 이렇게 연습을 반복해서 눈으로 읽지 않은 책이라도 '귀를 통해' 읽을 수 있을 정도가 되면, 리스닝으로 고생하는 일은 거의 없을 것입니다.

 왼쪽의 QR 코드를 스마트폰으로 인식하여 정식 오디오북을 들어 보세요! 더불어 롱테일북스 홈페이지(www.longtailbooks.co.kr)에서도 오디오북 MP3 파일을 다운로드 받을 수 있습니다.

스피킹(Speaking)이 고민이라면? 소리 내어 읽어 보세요!

스피킹 역시 많은 학습자들이 고민하는 부분입니다. 스피킹이 고민이라면, 원서를 큰 소리로 읽는 낭독 훈련(voice reading)을 해 보세요!

'소리 내어 읽는 것이 말하기에 정말로 도움이 될까?'라고 의아한 생각이 들 수도 있습니다. 하지만 인간의 두뇌 입장에서 봤을 때, 성대 구조를 활용해서 '발화'한다는 점에서는 소리 내어 읽기와 말하기에 큰 차이가 없다고 합니다. 소리 내어 읽는 것은 '타인의 생각'을 전달하고, 직접 말하는 것은 '자신의 생각'을 전달한다는 차이가 있을 뿐, 머릿속에서 문장을 처리하고 조음기관(혀와 성대 등)을 움직여 의미를 만든다는 점에서 같은 과정인 것이지요. 따라서 소리 내어 읽는 연습을 꾸준히 하는 것은 스피킹 연습에 큰 도움이 됩니다.

소리 내어 읽기를 하는 방법은 간단합니다. 일단 오디오북을 들으면서 성우의 목소리를 최대한 따라 하며 같이 읽어 보세요. 발음뿐 아니라 억양, 어조, 느낌까지 완벽히 따라 한다고 생각하면서 소리 내어 읽습니다. 따라 읽는 것이 조금 익숙해지면, 옆의 누군가에게 이 책을 읽어 준다는 생각으로 소리 내어 계속 읽어 나갑니다. 한 번 눈과 귀로 읽었던 책이기 때문에 보다 수월하게 진행할 수 있고, 자연스럽게 어휘와 표현을 복습하는 효과도 거두게 됩니다. 또 이렇게 소리 내어 읽은 것을 녹음해서 들어 보면 스스로에게도 좋은 피드백이 됩니다.

최근 말하기가 강조되면서 소리 내어 읽기가 크게 각광을 받고 있기는 하지만, 그렇다고 소리 내어 읽기가 무조건 좋은 것만은 아닙니다. 책을 소리 내어 읽다 보면, 무의식적으로 속으로 발음을 하는 습관을 가지게 되어 리딩 속도 자체는 오히려 크게 떨어지는 현상이 발생할 수 있습니다. 따라서 빠른 리딩 속도가 중요한 수험생이나 상위권 학습자들에게는 소리 내어 읽기가 적절하지 않은 방법입니다. 효과가 좋다는 말만 믿고 무턱대고 따라 하기보다는 자신의 필요에 맞게 우선순위를 정하고 원서를 활용하는 것이 좋습니다.

라이팅(Writing)까지 욕심이 난다면? 요약하는 연습을 해 보세요!

원서를 라이팅 연습에 직접적으로 활용하는 데에는 한계가 있지만, 적절히 활용하면 원서도 유용한 라이팅 자료가 될 수 있습니다.

특히 책을 읽고 그 내용을 요약하는 연습은 큰 도움이 됩니다. 요약 훈련의 방식도 간단합니다. 원서를 읽고 그날 읽은 분량만큼 혹은 책을 다 읽고 전체 내용을 기반으로, 책 내용을 한번 요약하고 나의 느낌을 영어로 적어 보는 것입니다.

이때 그 책에 나왔던 단어와 표현을 최대한 활용하여 요약하는 것이 중요합니다. 영어 표현력은 결국 얼마나 다양한 어휘로 많은 표현을 해 보았느냐가 좌우하게 됩니다. 이런 면에서 내가 읽은 책을, 그 책에 나온 문장과 어휘로 다시 표현해 보는 것은 매우 효율적인 방법입니다. 책에 나온 어휘와 표현을 단순히 읽고 무슨 말인지 아는 정도가 아니라, 실제로 직접 활용해서 쓸 수 있을 만큼 확실하게 익히게 되는 것이지요. 여기에 첨삭까지 받을 수 있는 방법이 있다면 금상첨화입니다.

이러한 '표현하기' 연습은 스피킹 훈련에도 그대로 적용될 수 있습니다. 책을 읽고 그 내용을 3분 안에 다른 사람에게 영어로 말하는 연습을 해 보세요. 순발력과 표현력을 기르는 좋은 훈련이 될 것입니다.

꾸준히 원서를 읽고 싶다면? 뉴베리 수상작을 계속 읽어 보세요!

뉴베리 상이 세계 최고 권위의 아동 문학상인 만큼, 그 수상작들은 확실히 완성도를 검증받은 작품이라고 할 수 있습니다. 특히 '쉬운 어휘로 쓰인 깊이 있는 문장'으로 이루어졌다는 점이 영어 학습자들에게 큰 호응을 얻고 있습니다. 이렇게 '검증된 원서'를 꾸준히 읽는 것은 영어 실력 향상에 큰 도움이 됩니다.

아래에 수준별로 제시된 뉴베리 수상작 목록을 보며 적절한 책들을 찾아 계속 읽어 보세요. 꼭 뉴베리 수상작이 아니더라도 마음에 드는 작가의 다른 책을 읽어 보는 것 또한 아주 좋은 방법입니다.

• 영어 초보자도 쉽게 읽을 만한 아주 쉬운 수준. 소리 내어 읽기에도 아주 적합.
Sarah, Plain and Tall★(Medal, 8,331단어), The Hundred Penny Box (Honor, 5,878단어), The Hundred Dresses★(Honor, 7,329단어), My Father's Dragon (Honor, 7,682단어), 26 Fairmount Avenue (Honor, 6,737단어)

• 중·고등학생 정도 영어 학습자라면 쉽게 읽을 수 있는 수준. 소리 내어 읽기에도 비교적 적합한 편.
Because of Winn-Dixie★(Honor, 22,123단어), What Jamie Saw (Honor, 17,203단어), Charlotte's Web (Honor, 31,938단어), Dear Mr. Henshaw (Medal, 18,145단어), Missing May (Medal, 17,509단어)

• 대학생 정도 영어 학습자라면 무난한 수준. 소리 내어 읽기에는 적합하지 않음.
Number The Stars★(Medal, 27,197단어), A Single Shard (Medal, 33,726단어), The Tale of Despereaux★(Medal, 32,375단어), Hatchet★(Medal, 42,328단어), Bridge to Terabithia (Medal, 32,888단어), A Fine White Dust (Honor, 19,022단어), Jennifer, Hecate, Macbeth, William McKinley and Me, Elizabeth (Honor, 23,266단어)

• 원서 완독 경험을 가진 학습자에게 적절한 수준. 소리 내어 읽기에는 적합하지 않음.
The Giver★(Medal, 43,617단어), From the Mixed-Up Files of Mrs. Basil E. Frankweiler (Medal, 30,906단어), The View from Saturday (Medal, 42,685단어), Holes★(Medal, 47,079단어), Criss Cross (Medal, 48,221단어), Walk Two Moons (Medal, 59,400단어), The Graveyard Book (Medal, 67,380단어)

뉴베리 수상작과 뉴베리 수상 작가의 좋은 작품을 엄선한 「뉴베리 컬렉션」에도 위 목록에 있는 도서 중 상당수가 포함될 예정입니다.

★ 「뉴베리 컬렉션」으로 이미 출간된 도서

어떤 책들이 출간되었는지 확인하려면, 지금 인터넷 서점에서
뉴베리 컬렉션을 검색해 보세요.

뉴베리 수상작을 동영상 강의로 만나 보세요!

영어원서 전문 동영상 강의 사이트 영서당(yseodang.com)에서는 뉴베리 컬렉션 『Holes』, 『Because of Winn-Dixie』, 『The Miraculous Journey of Edward Tulane』, 『Wayside School 시리즈』 등의 동영상 강의를 제공하고 있습니다. 뉴베리 수상작이라는 최고의 영어 교재와 EBS 출신 인기 강사가 만난 명강의! 지금 사이트를 방문해서 무료 샘플 강의를 들어 보세요!

'스피드 리딩 카페'를 통해 원서 읽기 습관을 길러 보세요!

일상에서 영어를 한마디도 쓰지 않는 비영어권 국가에서 살고 있는 우리가 영어 환경에 가장 쉽고, 편하고, 부담 없이 노출되는 방법은 바로 '영어원서 읽기'입니다. 언제 어디서든 원서를 붙잡고 읽기만 하면 곧바로 영어를 접하는 환경이 만들어지기 때문이지요. 하루에 20분씩만 꾸준히 읽는다면, 1년에 무려 120시간 동안 영어에 노출될 수 있습니다. 이러한 이유 때문에 영어 교육 전문가들이 영어원서 읽기를 추천하는 것이지요.

하지만 원서 읽기가 좋다는 것을 알아도 막상 꾸준히 읽는 것은 쉽지 않습니다. 그럴 때에는 13만 명 이상의 회원을 보유한 국내 최대 원서 읽기 동호회 〈스피드 리딩 카페〉(cafe.naver. com/readingtc)를 방문해 보세요.

원서별로 정리된 무료 PDF 단어장과 수준별 추천 원서 목록 등 유용한 자료는 물론, 뉴베리 수상작을 포함한 다양한 원서의 리뷰를 무료로 확인할 수 있습니다. 특히 함께 모여서 원서를 읽는 '북클럽'은 중간에 포기하지 않고 원서를 끝까지 읽는 습관을 기르는 데 큰 도움이 될 것입니다.

Answer Key

Chapter 1

1. A   Today, Monday, Wanda Petronski was not in her seat. But nobody, not even Peggy and Madeline, the girls who started all the fun, noticed her absence.

2. C   Nobody knew exactly why Wanda sat in that seat unless it was because she came all the way from Boggins Heights, and her feet were usually caked with dry mud that she picked up coming down the country roads. Maybe the teacher liked to keep all the children who were apt to come in with dirty shoes in one corner of the room.

3. D   Nobody knew exactly why Wanda sat in that seat unless it was because she came all the way from Boggins Heights, and her feet were usually caked with dry mud that she picked up coming down the country roads.

4. B   The reason Peggy and Maddie noticed Wanda's absence was because Wanda had made them late to school.

5. B   They had waited and waited for Wanda—to have some fun with her—and she just hadn't come.

6. D   They kept thinking she'd come any minute. They saw Jack Beggles running to school, his necktie askew and his cap at a precarious tilt. They knew it must be late, for he always managed to slide into his chair exactly when the bell rang as though he were making a touchdown.

7. C   The two girls reached their classroom after the doors had been closed. The children were reciting in unison the Gettysburg Address, for that was the way Miss Mason always began the session. Peggy and Maddie slipped into their seats just as the class was saying the last lines...

Chapter 2

1. C   After Peggy and Maddie stopped feeling like intruders in a class that had already begun, they looked across the room and noticed that Wanda was not in her seat.

2. D   Wanda lived way up on Boggins Heights, and Boggins Heights was no place to live. It was a good place to go and pick wildflowers in the summer, but you always held

your breath till you got safely past old man Svenson's yellow house.

3. D   "Wanda," Peggy would say in a most courteous manner, as though she were talking to Miss Mason or to the principal perhaps. "Wanda," she'd say, giving one of her friends a nudge, "tell us. How many dresses did you say you had hanging up in your closet?"

4. A   A hundred dresses! Obviously the only dress Wanda had was the blue one she wore every day. So what did she say she had a hundred for?

5. A   Peggy was not really cruel. She protected small children from bullies. And she cried for hours if she saw an animal mistreated. If anybody had said to her, "Don't you think that is a cruel way to treat Wanda?" she would have been very surprised. Cruel? What did the girl want to go and say she had a hundred dresses for? Anybody could tell that was a lie. Why did she want to lie? And she wasn't just an ordinary person, else why would she have a name like that? Anyway, they never made her cry.

6. B   As for Maddie, this business of asking Wanda every day how many dresses and how many hats and how many this and that she had was bothering her. Maddie was poor herself. She usually wore somebody's hand-me-down clothes. Thank goodness she didn't live up on Boggins Heights or have a funny name. And her forehead didn't shine the way Wanda's round one did. What did she use on it? Sapolio? That's what all the girls wanted to know.

7. C   But suppose Peggy and all the others started in on her next! She wasn't as poor as Wanda perhaps, but she was poor.

Chapter 3

1. D   A slight frown puckered her forehead. In the first place she didn't like being late to school. And in the second place she kept thinking about Wanda. Somehow Wanda's desk, though empty, seemed to be the only thing she saw when she looked over to that side of the room.

2. B   It was a bright blue day in September. No, it must, have been October, because when she and Peggy were coming to school, arms around each other and singing, Peggy had said, "You know what? This must be the kind of day they mean when they say, 'October's bright blue weather.'"

3. C   What they were all exclaiming about was the dress that Cecile had on—a crimson dress with cap and socks to match. It was a bright new dress and very pretty.

4. B   Everyone was admiring it and admiring Cecile. For long, slender Cecile was a toe dancer and wore fancier clothes than most of them. And she had her black satin bag with her precious white satin ballet slippers slung over her shoulders. Today was the day

say how wonderful the whole school thought she was, and please not to move away and everybody would be nice. She and Peggy would fight anybody who was not nice.

2. B   Maddie fell to imagining a story in which she and Peggy assailed any bully who might be going to pick on Wanda. "Petronski —Onski!" somebody would yell, and she and Peggy would pounce on the guilty one.

3. D   "I think that's where the Petronkis live," said Maddie, pointing to a little white house with lots of chicken coops at the side of it. Wisps of old grass stuck up here and there along the pathway like thin wet kittens. The house and its sparse little yard looked shabby but clean. It reminded Maddie of Wanda's one dress, her faded blue cotton dress, shabby but clean.

4. C   "Hey, Mr. Svenson!" yelled Peggy. "When did the Petronskis move?" Old man Svenson turned around, but said nothing. Finally he did answer, but his words were unintelligible, and the two girls turned and ran down the hill as fast as they could.

5. D   The Petronskis were gone. And now how could she and Peggy tell Wanda anything? Maybe the teacher knew where she had moved to. Maybe old man Svenson knew. They might knock on his door and ask on the way down. Or the post office might know. If they wrote a letter, Wanda might get it because the post office might forward it.

6. A   "Well, anyway," said Peggy, "she's gone now, so what can we do? Besides, when I was asking her about all of her dresses she probably was getting good ideas for her drawings. She might not even have won the contest otherwise."

7. A   She was never going to stand by and say nothing again. If she ever heard anybody picking on someone because they were funny looking or because they had strange names, she'd speak up. Even if it meant losing Peggy's friendship. She had no way of making things right with Wanda, but from now on she would never make anybody else so unhappy again. Finally, all tired out, Maddie fell asleep.

Chapter 7

1. A   It was just a friendly letter telling about the contest and telling Wanda she had won. They told her how pretty her drawings were, and that now they were studying about Winfield Scott in school. And they asked her if she liked where she was living now and if she liked her new teacher. They had meant to say they were sorry, but it ended up with their just writing a friendly letter, the kind they would have written to any good friend, and they signed it with lots of X's for love.

2. B   The minute they dropped the letter in the mailbox they both felt happier and more carefree.

3. C   After the party the teacher said she had a surprise, and she showed the class a

letter she had received that morning. "Guess who this is from," she said. "You remember Wanda Petronski? The bright little artist who won the drawing contest? Well, she has written me and I am glad to know where she lives because now I can send her medal. And I hope it gets there for Christmas. I want to read her letter to you."

4. D   "Dear Miss Mason: How are you and Room 13 ? Please tell the girls they can keep those hundred dresses because in my new house I have a hundred new ones all lined up in my closet. I'd like that girl Peggy to have the drawing of the green dress with the red trimming and her friend Maddie to have the blue one. For Christmas. I miss that school and my new teacher does not equalize with you. Merry Christmas to you and everybody. Yours truly, Wanda Petronski."

5. C   "Yes," said Peggy, holding her drawing out to look at it under the street lamp. "And boy! This shows she really liked us. It shows she got our letter and this is her way of saying that everything's all right. And that's that," she said with finality.

6. B   The colors in the dress were so vivid she had scarcely noticed the face and head of the drawing. But it looked like her, Maddie! It really did. The same short blond hair, blue eyes, and wide straight mouth. Why, it really looked like her own self! Wanda had really drawn this for her. Wanda had drawn her! In excitement she ran over to Peggy's.

7. D   "Look! She drew you. That's you!" she exclaimed. And the head and face of this picture did look like the auburn-haired Peggy. "What did I say!" said Peggy. "She must have really liked us anyway."

THE HUNDRED DRESSES

1판 1쇄   2016년 11월 14일
2판 2쇄   2024년 7월 15일

지은이 ELEANOR ESTES
기획 이수영
책임편집 김보경 정소이
콘텐츠제작및감수 롱테일 교육 연구소
저작권 명채린
마케팅 두잉글 사업 본부

펴낸이 이수영
펴낸곳 롱테일북스
출판등록 제2015-000191호
주소 04033 서울특별시 마포구 양화로 113, 3층(서교동, 순홍빌딩)
전자메일 help@ltinc.net

ISBN 979-11-91343-81-6 14740